WAJDAH

Ameen F. Rihani

WAJDAH

a play in four Acts

Platform International
Washington, DC

Ameen F. Rihani
WAJDAH
A play in Four Acts
Painting on cover by Khalil Saleeby
(with permission of Dr. Samir Saleeby)

First Edition 2001
Copyright © 2001 The Ameen Rihani Organization
Published by Platform International
Washington, DC

Library of Congress Control Number: 00-093505

ISBN: 0-96343-499-3

Acknowledgement:
Without the support of the Ministry of Culture in Lebanon the publication of this manuscript, as part of a series, would have not been possible.

Printed in Lebanon

Contents

○ Foreword 9

○ Characters 11

○ Principal Characters 13

○ Act I 16

○ Act II 43
  ❭ Scene I 43
  ❭ Scene II 52
  ❭ Scene III 56

○ Act III 66
  ❭ Scene I 66
  ❭ Scene II 73

○ Act IV 86
  ❭ Scene I 86
  ❭ Scene II 94

○ The English Works of
  Ameen F. Rihani 101

Foreword

At the dawn of the Twentieth Century, the young writer, Ameen Rihani, who became known as the father of Arab-American literature, wrote his first play in English, Wajdah. [Wajdah is perhaps the first English play written by an Arab-American.] The manuscript itself is not dated; however, Rihani mentions Wajdah in his English correspondence in 1908 and 1909. It can be assumed from the correspondence that he started writing this play in 1908 and completed it in 1909. (Rihani, Ameen Albert: Faylasuf-ul Furayka, --The Philosopher of Freike-- 1987, pp. 47-48; and Al-Yanabi' Al-Mansia, --Forgotten Springs-- 2000, p. 241).

Rihani's interest in theater started early in his life. When he was in his twenties, he joined the Henry Jewett acting group in New York. Rihani toured with this theatrical group as an actor and played roles in several Shakespearean plays. Rihani also spent many hours drawing sketches of the plays' main characters, Hamlet, Macbeth, Lady Macbeth, and others. The influence of this early phase of Rihani's life is clear in Wajdah. Powerful Shakespearean characters appear, such as "Lady" Wajdah, and there is a final scene with the unexpected deaths of the "Beloved." There is no doubt that Ameen Rihani was influenced by the plays he witnessed and in which he took part.

Rihani's uniqueness, however, is that he decided to create a play that addresses the history of the Arab World, articulated in English. Like its author, this play is the product of both worlds.

Wajdah, the heroine of the play, is a Yemeni Princess of the seventh century who converts to Islam and faces the challenge of reconciling faith and reason. The conflict is brought about by the disappearance of her infant son during a religious battle in Arabia. After many years, a young man is presented as her son and she is in turmoil about his true identity. Her endless search for the truth makes her struggle more significant. Unbearable emotional and mental pain torments her. Wajdah's faith is deeply wounded and her reasoning is profoundly shaken. Wajdah contemplates running away to the desert where she thinks she will find rebirth, liberty, and a purified soul. The tragic ending of the play is reminiscent of some Shakespearean endings and reflects the dramatic results of wars.

The play's innovative aspect is that it seeks to convey to Western readers a topic that is neither familiar nor usual to them . This may be the first time that Islamic history is presented to the English reader in a play. Perhaps it is the first time that an Arab-American portrays to the West a defiant Arab woman from the seventh century who questions everything, and defies all norms. Rihani has been known for successfully and eloquently bringing together two cultural poles. In addition, in Wajdah, he brings together the unexpected.

The publication of Wajdah, more than ninety years since it was written, marks how a new literary genre, a play written in 1908 about Arab history in the English language, was created.

Finally, it is worthwhile to mention that this book is published as part of a larger project with the objective of publishing all Rihani's English manuscripts. *Critiques in Art* was the first book in this series, issued in 1999; *Wajdah* is the second book, with the hope to continue publishing all existing manuscripts until all the Rihani unpublished English work becomes available to the reader locally and overseas.

The Publisher

NB: The term "manuscript" in the case of this play, Wajdah, may not apply accurately because it does not carry the meaning of a handwritten text. It is a typewritten text of 88 pages on old beige and thin paper. Two of these pages carry a repeated number: 39a, 39b, and 46a, 46b. The play then becomes a manuscript of 90 pages. There is no explanation to these, supposedly, typing mistakes. Prior to the text we find three pages, with roman numbers, introducing the characters. The number of verses in each page varies between 24 and 27 verse, except for the first and last page of each of the four acts where the number of verses drops down to somewhere between 12 and 18. Most corrections and, or changes, are typewritten and very few are handwritten. (Rihani, Ameen Albert, Al-Yanabi' Al-Mansia --Forgotten Springs--, 2000, pp. 241-246).

Characters

IMAM ALI   (Im' am" A' li" or A" li') The Khalif

ABBAS   (Ab' bas") Friend of Ali

ABU-MOUSA   (A" bu' Mou" sa') Friend of Ali

AHMED   (Ah" med') Ali's Scribe

MUSTAFA   (Mus" ta' fa' or Mus' ta" fa')
A wealthy citizen of Koufah

KICE   (Kice") Mustafa's adopted son

GANNAM   (Gan' nam") Once a slave of Wajdah's

HUMMAD   (Hum' mad") Armorer

SHEIBAN   (Shei' ban") Armorer

TABTABA   (Tab" ta' ba') Poet and water-carrier

KLEIB   (Kleib") Captain of the Guards

OBEID   (O' beid") a gaoler

A MESSENGER

MAHMOUD   (Mah" moud' or Mah' moud") Slave of Wajdah

ZEID   (Zeid") Slave of Wajdah

WAJDAH   (Waj" dah') Wife of Mustafa and supposed real Mother of Kice

SALWAH   (Sal" wah') Servant of Wajdah

LABIBAH   (Labi" bah') Servant of Wajdah

SCENE: KOUFAH and the DESERT

TIME: Seventh Century A.D.

Note: ei in Zeid, Obeid, Kleib, like a in fade

MOAWIA   (Mo' a" wi' a') The enemy of Ali (Mentioned in the Play)

Principal Characters

WAJDAH: She is about forty years of age, of magnificent physique, tall
           and commanding, dark-complexioned, more magnetic than
           beautiful. Born a pagan princess, she was brought up in her
           native hills of Yemen to love the open air, the hunt and the
           beauties of nature. She could throw the javelin like an expert;
           was noted for horsemanship, and more than once fought in
           battle, after she became a Mohammedan. She was conquered,
           rather converted by Ali. Yemen, where her father ruled
           before it was conquered by Islam, is that part of Arabia that
           was noted for its woven materials, its spices, and its Jinn. In
           ancient times the people of Yemen were called "weavers and
           tanners and drivers of goblins." Wajdah has lapses of
           paganism, and is superstitious. Her passions and her
           reactions are equally intense.
           She dresses in flowing silk robes, rather meagerly at home, of
           brilliant coloring; wears Oriental jewelry, such as long
           ear-rings of filigree gold, heavy bracelets of silver, anklets, a
           ring and a necklace of carnelian stones. Her hair is done in
           two long plaits; her feet are shod with sandals ornamented
           with beads. When she goes out, she wears a loose fitting
           cloak, much like that of the men, covers her head with a
           mantle over which she ties across her brows in a coquettish
           angle a sash of satin or silk. She is never veiled.

IMAM ALI: A warrior, orator, and poet, he is one of the heroes and
           leading lights of Islam. He fought many battles with the
           Prophet himself, and made many conquests for the Faith both
           with the sword and his persuasive eloquence. He is
           outspoken and uncompromising, simple of manners and
           rather conscious of his spiritual superiority. More of a
           warrior than a politician, and more of a poet and sage than a
           warrior, his political ambition was never wholly realized.
           Nevertheless, he remained steadfast to his lofty principles to
           the last and was always a magnanimous and pathetic figure.

13

He was at the time of the Play about sixty years of age. He dressed like an ascetic, wearing plain sandals, a cotton tunic, and his sword hung from his shoulder by a cord made of hemp. He carried a staff in the street and wore over his tunic an **aba**, cloak, made of camel hair. His turban is a light green, the color of the Prophet and his descendants.
Imam is his religious title.

ABBAS: He is about Ali's age, but dyes and trims his beard and looks ten years younger. A man of action, he is self-willed and commanding, although subtle and shrewd, in pursuing his course. He affects a bluff and burly manner. He dresses somewhat gaudily, say, his tunic is of striped material, his **aba** trimmed with gold, his pointed, heel-less shoes of dark green or red leather. He carries a sword.

ABU-MOUSA: An old man of about seventy five, with flowing beard. The Nestor of that period, he is Ali's chief adviser, as gentle and soft-spoken as he is wise. He wears a white tunic with a dark-colored sash across his waste, a cloak cut like a gabardine, preferably black, a large white turban, and sandals. He carries a staff.

MUSTAFA: He is about sixty years old, of flagmatic temperament. He trims and dies his beard; walks with shoulders and head bowed; and has a sly look. He dresses in silks of brilliant colors, the tunic of striped material, the cloak of solid color trimmed with gold. Instead of a turban he wears the usual kerchief,--his is of silk and tasseled,--overwhich is pressed a heavy black cord. Such head-gear is called by the Arabs **koufiyeh** and **aghal**, and is worn by everyone, except the learned and the religious leaders. Both the **koufieyh** and **aghal** are of different materials, silk, cotton, coarse wool, etc.

KICE: (Pronounced like Rice) He is twenty two years of age, an impetuous and reckless youth, honest, forthright, outspoken, and very handsome. He dresses like his step-father in costly silks of brilliant colors, wears pointed red boots instead of sandals, and carries a sword.

14

AHMED: He is about Kice's age, but of a weak nature, timid and equivocating. He is also handsome, but dresses more simply, living as he does in Ali's house and partly conforming, outwardly at least, to his Master's humor. His tunics--he must have two or three changes--are of cotton material, his **abas** of camel hair, his head-gears of silk, but subdued in color. He wears black boots and carries a sword.

TABTABA: A man about fifty, ascetic in habits, extravagant in speech. He is a professional rhymster and rhetorician, with a flow of words that often overcomes his thought and drowns his wit. He is a privileged character, who speaks his mind always, and to everyone. He wears an open tunic of indigo blue cotton cloth, which he shortens by tucking it at the waist under a leather belt, thus baring his legs as well as his bosom. He sometimes wears an aba of coarse wool, and gives himself the privilege in the city of wearing a turban. He goes bare-footed, and when he is not carrying the water-skin, he carries a staff. His beard is short, but grows in abandon.

Wajdah

. . . .

ACT I

Public Square in Koufah: a crouching place for camels with two palm trees and a large earthen basin for water near them. Houses, flat-roofed and thatched, to left and right, with entrances. An arch-way corner leading to the Mosque, whose minaret--practicable--rises in the rear. An open view showing part of City wall and palm groves on horizon. A well in the centre of the Square with an earthen jar tied to a rope. Well practicable.

Time: Morning, flush of dawn.

In the MINARET the MUAZZEN is calling the Faithful to the morning prayer.

MUAZZEN   **Allahu akbar, Allahu akbar!**

               La ilaha illallah, la ilaha illallah![1]

               (CITIZENS pass in their way to the MOSQUE

               Enter HUMMAD, SHEIBAN and other ARMORERS in their working clothes.)

HUMMAD   And this will also be
               A year of blood and steel.

SHEIBAN   And for the armorers prosperity.
               Allah's slaves the armorers must live.

HUMMAD   Thy neighbor's curse thy blessing then shall be.

---

1. Translation: God is almighty, God is almighty! God is all, God is all!
   Literally: God is most great, God is most great!
   There is no God but he, there is no God but he!
   (the translation and literally words are written by the author)

SHEIBAN	Allah is all-seeing and all-wise-- Allah be praised!
HUMMAD	But wait till thou art paid. Thy pious hope might yet bark at thy heels For bread. (Drums heard) Hear that. It is for thee, for me, For all of us. (Enter an old Sheikh)
SHEIKH	By the god of the Kaaba! Is this a call to prayer or a call to arms!
HUMMAD	To both, my reverend sheikh.
SHEIKH	It can not be.
HUMMAD	Why not? What we can not in prayer amend, The sword in combat can.
SHEIKH	Allah forfend!
SHEIBAN	But our Emirs...
SHEIKH	May Allah guide them now. Alas, that they should squander thus the blood Of our young nation. Arabia wants peace. Allah send us peace. (Exit)
HUMMAD	If he does not, Then we must work, and for the Prophet's sake.
SHEIBAN	Upon him peace! But if he wants a war, I say the war will be.
HUMMAD	(To two of his men) But will you work? Will you accept the Khalif's word for pay?

MEN	No more, no more.
HUMMAD	(Turning to the crowd) And you, O brother Arabs? Has any of you yet received in coin A **dirhem**[1] for his labor from the State!
FIRST A.	Not I, billah![2]
SECOND A.	Nor I.
THIRD A.	Nor I.
FOURTH A.	Nor I.
HUMMAD	Has any of you ever received a spoil Or even a rusty a spear-head of a spoil For working day and night to serve the State?
ALL	No, never, billah! no.
HUMMAD	And will you thus Continue as the creditors of Faith While at your heels the dogs of hunger bark?
ALL	No, billah, no.
SHEIBAN	(To himself) The armorers must live.
HUMMAD	Attend, therefore, and open well your eyes. 'T is rumored that the enemy of Ali Has recently enlisted in his service The magic coffers of the Princess Wajdah. Now, whether Ali or Moawia pays, Or Wajdah or her husband Mustafa, It is the same with us.

---

1. The basic monetary unit in Koufah in the Seventh Century A.D.
2. billah meaning in the name of God.

SHEIBAN   But I think not
That Wajdah cares a coin about this war.
I hear that she and Kice--and no one knows
Whether he be her lover or her son--
Are set on fleeing old Mustafa's home.

HUMMAD   She might be going to Moawia...
But that concerns us not.
Be this, therefore, our word, our final word:
We seek no spoils, we hanker for no trophies;
But we will not submit to requisition,
Nor give our labor, for the Prophet's sake,
Free to the State,
As freely as we did before.

ALL   Nay, billah, nay.

HUMMAD   Then say to our Emeers:
Give us silver and we will give you steel.

ALL   Life of Allah! yes.

SHEIBAN   And say this too:
We're free to sell to whomsoever pays.

ALL   Aye, billah, aye!

SHEIBAN   Be it Moawia,
Or Mustafa or Wajdah, or Ali.

ALL   Aye, billah, aye!

(Enter Abbas and Ahmed)

ABBAS   And what's amiss, O Arabs?
Why these clamors at the break of dawn?

HUMMAD   Because our wrongs in these tumultuous days

Will not be heard elsewise,--because our claims,--

ABBAS	What are your claims? what are your wrongs?
HUMMAD	Life of Allah! Have we yet been paid, O good Abbas, a **dirhem** for our labors! For making arms, And scouring arms, And repairing arms, And forging arms To fight the foes of Islam and the State! If we are then to have another war, As do the drums this early morn presage, We can not furnish any arms until The Khalif pays--
SHEIBAN	(Ingratiatingly) the armorers must live.
ABBAS	Rest ye assured, for though the Faithful owe A moiety of their labor to the Faith, Yet shall you be upheld in all your claims And made content.
HUMMAD	Even with like words Our grievances were mollified before. We go however to our morning prayer In hope that what the honored Abbas said Will stand the test of truth.
SHEIBAN	One can not work Forever without recompense at all.
HUMMAD	No, not a weapon until we are paid.
ALL	Aye, give us silver and we will give you steel. (Exeunt)
ABBAS	That argues ill; for if the armorers Are now become so indurate and bold,

So tainted with the lust of pelf withal,
Rebellion prospers even in our Koufah.

AHMED   But there must be an instigating hand,--
         Someone who, in the name of labor, decks
         Treachery to make it seem attractive.

ABBAS   Decks it with silver, eh?

AHMED   Indeed, and gold.
         They've had a taste of money; otherwise,
         They would not, like a baby in the tantrums,
         Cry for it with such drooling petulance.

ABBAS   Thou speakest with conviction; thou must know
         The sources of seduction.

AHMED   I know this:
         Wherever they be, they are not of Islam.
         The recreants, the infidels, that would
         Instil their poison in a Moslem's heart,
         Are enemies of Allah and the Prophet.

ABBAS   And might they not be lurking, like a snake,
         In some dark cranny of a friendly wall?

AHMED   Show me the wall, and I will turn the stone,
         Aye, every stone in it to find the snake.

ABBAS   Be not too quick and sure. The recreants
         Who now corrupt our armorers with gold,
         Turning them to hirelings and traitors,
         Are in this city. Yea, and it may be
         That thou, O Ahmed--

AHMED   (Showing surprise) Pray, what dost thou mean?
         Why look upon me thus?

ABBAS	And art thou not Often within the wall--
AHMED	What wall? Wouldst say--?
ABBAS	The cranny, I would say, where lies the snake.
AHMED	(Changing his tone) And why this cryptic turn?
ABBAS	(In a rebuking manner) As if thy mind Had not already caught, and dwelled upon, My own intention. I would say, young man, That Wajdah is the snake.
AHMED	It can not be.
ABBAS	(Stroking his beard) And wouldst thou wheedle even with Abbas? I know thy mind and somewhat of thy heart. But this is not the time for dalliance.
AHMED	(Disconcerted) For what?
ABBAS	Come now, be free and frank with me. For though thou hide thy love from all the world, Thou canst not hide it from the man who shared With thee thy tent--and heard these in they dream.
AHMED	(With plaintive confidence that develops into the fervor of conviction). By Allah! I am weary of it all. I long to be again among the tribes Of my own land where, in my infant days, Arabia cherished friendliness and peace. I'm weary of the dark abodes of State, Where love is poisoned for the sake of power. Aye, if the Fates would favor my design, I'd run away this very day from Koufah, Even as I did from distant Teyma once...

23

It has been ever thus with me, alas!
Whenever I fall in love, I run away.

ABBAS   Thine honor must prevail, else thou art not
The man in whom the Khalif put his trust.

AHMED   The Khalif? Dear with me, O good Abbas.
If to unbosom to a friend has aught
Of solace in it, I must thank thee now;
For I would bare my heart to none but thee.
In Teyma, where I learned to read the poems
In which the heroes of Arabia live
Forever to inspire us to deeds
Of bravery and sacrifice, I was
First taught to love, and shrine in memory,
My father and my mother: they both fell
In battle fighting 'gainst the great Ali.
My slave Gannam--O where art thou to-day?
Would that I could hear thee again relate
Of how my mother fought against Ali,
And how she fell a victim to--his sword
Or moral power, I know not.
Howbeit, I am loyal to the Khalif.
Life of this day! I am. But I can, too.
Be loyal to the woman thou dost call
A reptile. O, my honored Sheikh, be just.
The Princess Wajdah has no secret hand
In any plot, I swear, against the State,
Or any of Moawia's machinations.

ABBAS   But openly--

AHMED   Aye, Mustafa and Kice
Are openly opposing the Imam.

ABBAS   But Kice, thou knowest, is a callow youth,
And Mustafa his father is a dotard.
How can the wretched twain be leading minds
In plots against the State or the Imam?

24

	I tell thee they are instruments of one Who is the moving power.
AHMED	(With emphasis) That is true; But in Damascus is the moving power. Moawia is the backbone of Mustafa.
ABBAS	(Dubiously) And Kice?
AHMED	He's but an echo, although he Is one of those who would incriminate Ali in the assassination of The Khalif Othman.
ABBAS	(Ruminating) I was told that once He put thee out of Wajdah's house.
AHMED	Not so. (Enter MUSTAFA and KICE) But here he is; I challenge him to tell The truth.
ABBAS	O Sheikh Mustafa, why in haste?
MUSTAFA	(Pretending not to have seen them.) Peace on thee, Sheikh Abbas, and Ahmed, peace! Is't true, the rumor of another war?
ABBAS	Yes, if Moawia and his friends desire. For who, with but a thought of Arab honor, Can tolerate the wicked machinations Of these high-stomached, hollow-hearted men? Who, with the fire of Islam in his breast, Will suffer those that gave not the Imam Their suffrage, to add infamy to ill By thus accusing him of Othman's death?
MUSTAFA	A heavy accusation that, indeed.

25

ABBAS	And one that should be silenced with the sword.
KICE	But what if it be true?
ABBAS	If it be true?
KICE	Aye, what if it be true? (Somewhat defiant)
MUSTAFA	(Apart to Kice) Hush, hush!
ABBAS	There is No truth, my boy, where malice dominates And selfishness is judge.
KICE	(Drawing away from Mustafa) But wouldst thou doubt The proof when it is clearer than this dawn?
MUSTAFA	(Taking hold of Kice.) Silence, Allah curse thee! Silence, now. (To Abbas) O Sheikh Abbas, let not his prattle tax Thine earnest spirit.
KICE	(Snatching his sleeve away from Mustafa's hand) Life of Allah! Might not an Arab freely speak his mind?
AHMED	(To Mustafa) I pray thee, let him speak.--Continue, Kice, And give thy tongue free rein to suit thy heart.
KICE	(Ignoring Ahmed) A wound, when in the dressing 'tis exposed, Revives the dormant pain, O Sheikh Abbas. And so a suffering heart. For whether false or true the accusation, Which now finds in this city willing tongues, Is big with ill and woe to all Islam. But hear, and may my tongue cleave to my mouth If I speak falsely, Yesternight, my Sheikh, As I was coming from the Mosque, I passed

By Ali's house, and billah! heard a voice
Among the palms--it cried out twice, I swear!
"Beware, O Khalif of they Scribe, beware!"

ABBAS   And what wouldst thou insinuate by this?

AHMED   What signifies the tale?

KICE   Thou knowest well.
The Khalif need not go out of his house
To find the traitors.

MUSTAFA   (Dragging Kice away) Allah's curse upon thee!

ABBAS   We'd know the truth, Mustafa; let him speak.

AHMED   And be thou clear.

KICE   This man, O Sheikh Abbas,
Has told my mother that he can not now,
Because of what he knows, remain in office.

AHMED   That is not true.

KICE   Let her be questioned then.
But didst thou not want her to leave with thee,--
To go away from Koufah! (Mustafah is amazed)
Didst thou not
Try to empoison her against her son
And husband?

AHMED   Churl accursed! a liar base!

KICE   But who is likelier to fit they words,
He who can boast of the most noble strains,
Or he who might be but a come-by-chance?

AHMED   By Allah, this shall prove my noble birth.
(Draws his sword)

KICE	But, like thy tongue, thy steel is false. The proof? (Rushes at him with his sword)
ABBAS	(Raising his hand in command) Forbear, Ahmed; and thou Kice, sheathe thy sword.
MUSTAFA	(Drawing Kice away) I'd cut thy tongue off for thy dung of words. Wilt ruin us, thou foul!--O Sheikh Abbas, O Ahmed, pray, forget this and forgive.
KICE	By Allah and the Prophet!--
MUSTAFA	Come, come hence.
ABBAS	And this remember, O Sheikh Mustafa: We count upon thy zeal and sterling worth. Thou hast been a true Moslem in the past; Be not to-day the contrary. Salaam!
MUSTAFA	Allah forfend!--Salaam. (Exit MUSTAFA and KICE)
ABBAS	(In solemn tone) Ahmed! Look thou into this sacred face of dawn And swear that thou art innocent of aught The Princess Wajdah has against Islam.
AHMED	By All that flows from Allah's hand, I swear That my relations with the Princess Wajdah Are free from aught that menaces Islam;-- I swear-- (Enter IMAM ALI, ABOU-MOUSA, KLEIB and others attending.)
ABBAS	Enough. Peace be with the Imam.

ALI   And Allah's peace upon you, and his blessings.
                   How fares our cousin Sheikh Abbas to-day?

ABBAS   As this ill-fated and dismembered nation.

ALI   But we are in the dawning of Islam.
                   What still remains of darkness on the hills
                   And in the valleys, soon must pass away.

ABBAS   The contrary. For those who yesterday
                   Followed the Prophet, fought beneath his standard,--
                   Those who oft swore by Ali's head, are now
                   Disbanded, disaffected, malcontent,--
                   Rebellious 'gainst their ruler and their god.[1]

ALI   And are such matters alien to our ken?
                   Should we now fear the jungles, where we oft
                   Planted our darts in mad rebellious breasts
                   And saw them growing in succeeding years
                   To beautiful, fruit-bearing trees of faith?
                   Are not our eyes accustomed to behold
                   The stout horns of rebellion rise and lunge?
                   But have we not plucked out the very fangs
                   Of many a prowling and soft-footed intrigue?
                   Why, then, with doubt and fear, O Sheikh Abbas,
                   Wouldst thou untie in the believer's breast
                   The knot of faith and valor?

ABBAS   O Ali,
                   Rebellion's brewing even here in Koufah;--
                   Yea, in this virgin city, Allah's foes,
                   Through our most dear but questionable friends,
                   Are new corrupting with silver and gold
                   The simplest of the children of Islam.

ALI   What dost thou mean.

---

1. With small "g" as in original text

29

ABBAS   The armorers, it seems,
             Have tasted of Moawia's gold.

ALI   (Somewhat annoyed) But how?

ABBAS   Through Wajdah or Mustafa. Wajdah's house
             Is Moawia's base of action here in Koufah;--
             It is a hive of intrigue.

ALI   (Imperturbed) Wajdah's house?
             Naught that is least unfriendly to Islam
             Can come from Wajdah's house.

ABU-MOUSA   (Who had been reading a parchment, and laughing)
             But look at this,-- (Offering it to Ali)
             I picked it up this morning at my door,
             And I believe it comes from Wajdah's house.
             I know the rhymster's manner; it is he
             The water-carrier of Princess Wajdah,
             Who writes such squibs for hire.

ABBAS   Tabtaba?

ABU-MOUSA   The very one, I trow.

ALI   Read it to us.

ABU-MOUSA   (Reading) "The year our hero came to power, my son,
                         Is what is called a year of hemorrhages;
                     Which argues well his reign a bloody one,
                         Despite the auguries of fools and sages.
                     But whether Hashem or Omaiyah bleed,--
                         Whether Irak shall triumph or Esh-Sham,
                     The hand of fate will break the winning reed
                         And clothe with guilty purple al-Islam.
                     For Ali the destroyer of battalions
                         Is now forsooth a leader of rapscallions."
                     The rap is on thy men, not on thyself.

30

(He hands parchment to Ali)
(TABTABA appears carrying on his back a water-skin)

ALI   (Glancing over the verses)
               There's more than mere buffoonery in this.

ABBAS   Here is the poet; ask him.

ALI   Tabtaba,
               Come hither.

TABTABA   (Coming down stage) Peace upon Imam Ali.

ALI   Upon all true believers, Allah's peace.
               Read this, and make true answer to our question.

TABTABA   Permit me first to lay this down, and then--
               As one should stand in thy most noble presence.
               (He lays down the water-skin and stands upright, his hands
               folded on his breast.)
               Now I can freely breathe to voice the truth.
               Thy bidding, O Imam.

ALI   (Handing parchment) Read this.

TABTABA   (Casts a glance at it, shakes his head and refuses to take it.)
               Thy pardon--
               I can not read it.

ALI   Why!

TABTABA   (Making a gesture of contempt) Because it's mine.

ALI   Translate to us, therefore, the prattle of
               This daughter of thy fancy.

TABTABA   Not a daughter, O most honored Imam, but a boy of my
               fancy.
               In truth, a she-brat I would never own. I would cast it away,

31

burn it, or bury it alive. But are not the masculinities of this one, even as thy slave's before thee, strongly featured in the lines?

Are they not prominent enough, even protrusive in their place?

Although in Koufah there be more mawkish minions of the rhyme than swordsmen or herdsmen or grammarians, whence but from the loins of my genius could this have issued? Its prattle? One does not mistake the bulbul's notes, or the dove's cooing, or the bray of the lion, especially if one is a poet like the Imam. Although I have heard it said by those who are called bards by their hinds and their nearest kin and who bring forth only squealing she-brats, blubbered and deformed, that the rhymes of the Imam are woefully commonplace.

ABU-MOUSA His insolence and his garrulity
Would seem to be competing for a prize.

ALI (Amused) Who instigated this? Who hired thee?

TABTABA What thou callest instigation, I call inspiration. A certain one comes to me with a tale of woe or the contrary of it; or with a grievance against one of thine officials or the contrary of it; or with an amorous paroxism or the contrary of it;--I listen attentively, sitting thus reverentially in the august presence of my genius,
(He sits down cross--legged, bows his head and places his palms upon his knees.) and if I am inspired or instigated,...it matters not which,
I send my patron the next day a ringing poem and he sends his slave to me with a ringing purse. The which I accept, O noble Imam, not in the way thou callest "hired to do it", but in conformity to a proverb current that only the niggardly refuse a largess, only the base one refuses a present. And I kiss my hand every day (He rises, kissing the back and the palm of his hand) in praise of Allah that being neither niggardly nor base, I must accept whatever is sent to me.

ALI   And art thou finished?
            (Tabtaba nods, waving his hand)
            Who rewarded thee?

TABTABA   By Allah and the Prophet, I can not say.

ALI   Not even if we command thee?

TABTABA   To break faith with my patron, never! Not if thou cut my
            weasend, never, never! I swear by all that's sacred to a right
            Moslem to make my breast the grave of all such secrets.

ABBAS   That such a grave should thus be sanctified.

AHMED   And how impenetrable is the churl.

ABU-MOUSA   And yet, how shallow-honest.

ALI   Very well,
            We shall not force thee to forswear thyself.
            But tell us the true meaning of this line:
            "And clothe with guilty purple al-Islam."

TABTABA   And dare I explain to one who is many orbits above me in
            poesy, and many zones beyond me in discernment, and many
            circles below me in learning? Thou knowest what is meant by
            guilty, and thou surely canst tell purple from black or yellow.
            Now, of thee and Moawia, who is to be the tailor of Islam,
            Allah knows, not I.

ABBAS   And that is the putrescence of the grave.
            Thy breast of secrets stinks. Be off!
            (While Tabtaba was speaking, Abu-Mousa whispered
            something into Ali's ear. But Ali shook his head and waved
            his hand, ordering Tabtaba away, just as Abbas had said "Be
            off" Tabtaba makes a gesture of obeisance and is about to
            make a speech of thanks, when a noise and a confusion of
            voices are heard within.)

ABU-MOUSA   What noise be this!

ABBAS   The armorers again.

             (Enter A MESSENGER pursued by a crowd of citizens.)

FIRST C.   Slit the bastard's nose before you kill him.

SECOND C.   Cut off his tongue before you cut his halse!

ABU-MOUSA   Enough!

ABBAS   Forbear!

AHMED   Stand back!

ALI   And who be this?

FIRST C.   A messenger from Moawia, he says.

SECOND C.   A dog, a pig!--

ALI   Have done! Now brother Arab,
             Whence comest and what hast thou? Speaks--come forth.

MESSENGER   (Advancing) I have a message from Moawia
             To Ali son of Abi-Taleb.

ALI   Well,
             Thy message.

MESSENGER   Thou the son of Abi-Taleb?

AHMED   (To Messenger) Say, Peace on the Imam.

MESSENGER   (Handing the Message to Ali) I am commanded
             To say to thee that sixty thousand Arabs
             Have risen in Damascus to avenge
             The murdered Khalif, and they want the blood

Of Ali [son of] Abi-Taleb for the crime.
(The crowd threaten the Messenger)

ALI   Molest him not; he's but a messenger
Who's faithful to his charge.
Say to Moawia, O brother Arab,
That our reply is not what he may read,
But what he shall behold, and very soon.
Stay; give him an order of safe conduct, Kleib,
And see that he's protected through the city.

(Exeunt Kleib, Messenger and some citizens.)

Ahmed, bid Wajdah come to us at once.

(Exit Ahmed)

Speak to the armorers, O Sheikh Abbas;
Tell them they shall be paid--we must have arms.

(Exit Abbas)

And Abu-Mousa, go among the people
And with thy wonted mellowness of tongue
Season the bitterness of discontent.
Arabia once more must show her steel
An justify her faith.
(To the crowd)
Go forth, my friends,
And each one be an echo of the voice
That calls you now to arms and the **jehad.**[1]

(Exeunt Ali and Abu-Mousa and Citizens in different directions.)

TABTABA   (Alone) To arms, ye fools, and then--to paradise! A houri 's worth a spear; and some, they say, are worth a dozen. Another **jehad**, forsooth! and the worms will feast upon the spoils of Death. But where do the houris come in? and when? After the feast is over? A spear, a corpse, a worm, a bone, an abyss, a houri--is that the alphabet of the universe? Well,

---

1. or jihad meaning a holy war as a religious duty.

well--but why trouble my poor head about it. The city will soon be empty, and Tabtaba will have a rest. O War, "I know that in thy spear,..." how did I begin that poem? "I know that in thy spear, O war, Is wisdom from a distant star." A wretched world, a crowded world, a rat-hole of a world 't would be'--another good line--If you did not come now and then to sweep and clean,--to sweep and clean--to sweep and clean--and give us a little elbow room. I'll get the rhyme yet. What I really want to say is that we'd eat each other, billah, if we did n't butcher each other every now and then. But why trouble your poor head, O Tabtaba, about it.

(Draws water from the well to fill his water-skin and sings)

I was asleep when Eblis came
Into my tent his tithe to claim.
He pinched me hard and whispered low,--
"Every deer must have a doe."
--"But I have not, alas, for joy!"
--"Hast thou not then a soft-cheeked boy?"
--I am alone."--Thou soul of soot,
Hast thou not then a lyre or lute?"
--"I do not play."--"Thou haberdine,
Hast thou not even a little wine?"
--"I do not drink."--"Then sleep for good,
Thou art but a block of wood!"

And the devil never came after that; for being sure of thrice his tithes in the other world, he is exceedingly indulgent with us poets here. And even our Prophet Mohammed connives in this. In very truth, the Apostle of Allah likes not the poets. We rove blindly everywhere, he says, and are followed only by the deluded and distraught. So says the Prophet. Mercy on his beard, me likes him not for that. And though he orders the gates of Paradise shut in my face, me likes him not. Ah, but the houris will intercede for the poets. And what can the Prophet do, when the dark-eyed, ravishing ones press around him and cry: O, let the poets in, or let us out!

(Citizens pass returning from the Mosque.
TABTABA is filling his water-skin while a flower-girl
passes singing:)

"Here are flowers, O my Beloved,
  Here are flowers;
Let us lay our hearts to-day
  Among the flowers.
Let us not be led astray
  By the mirage far away,--
Here is verdure, and in verdure
  Love embowers."

TABTABA (Carries water-skin and goes out singing)
"Here are springs, O my Beloved,
  Here are springs;
Let us rest and build our nest
  Near the springs.
Let us cease our weary quest
  For the mountains of the blest;
Here is water, and in water
  Blessings sings.

(Re-enter Ali, AHMED and KLEIB)

ALI (Reading a parchment)---And what you spend on arms in Koufah will not be spent in vain--...pay them in gold...be assured of the governership of Egypt for Kice....

How comest thou, O Kleib, by this?

KLEIB We searched

The messenger.

ALI (To Ahmed) And dost thou think that Wajdah Would countenace a treason? (He sits on a stone near the well.)

AHMED Billah, no.
But here she is to answer for herself.

37

(Enter Wajdah, stands before Ali who remains seated, but does not look at Ahmed or Kleib, who retire and converse apart.)

ALI

Peace on thee Wajdah.

WAJDAH

And on thee, Ali, peace.
Thy wish.

ALI

For fifteen years thou hast been loyal,
O Wajdah, to Islam and Ali.

WAJDAH

Well.

ALI

And with thy tongue and arm and heart and wealth
Thou didst uphold the word of Allah.

WAJDAH

Well.

ALI

Well. Wilt thou with apostasy now crown
Thy noble work and life?

WAJDAH

What dost thou mean?

ALI

(Handing parchments) Read this--and this.

WAJDAH

(Reads and returns them to Ali) I do not understand.

ALI

But this was written by Tabtaba.

WAJDAH

Even so.

ALI

And Tabtaba is of thy hinds.

WAJDAH

Even so.

ALI

And hinds have no mind of their own.

WAJDAH	In this I'm of thy mind.
ALI	Therefore, this Tabtaba Is but an instrument, as he avowed; But in whose hand invisible is he? Who instigated this?
WAJDAH	I can not say.
ALI	Thou knowst and wouldst not say?
WAJDAH	I do not know.
ALI	But this comes from thy house. I doubt not that. And thou wilt, therefore, answer for it.
WAJDAH	I?
ALI	Who else? who but the master of the house?
WAJDAH	And when was woman master of her house?
ALI	Eigh! wilt thou quibble with thy friend Ali!
WAJDAH	And wilt thou thus suspect thy friend Wajdah?
ALI	But I know well thy husband.
WAJDAH	(With a shrug of the shoulder) I have none.
ALI	What dost thou mean?
WAJDAH	(Deliberately) I mean I have no husband.
ALI	Thou speak'st in riddles.

WAJDAH	Life of Allah, no.
ALI	Explain, therefore.
WAJDAH	Hadst thou not sent for me, I would have come to thee for that.
ALI	(Impatient) For what?
WAJDAH	(In a calm manner) For what thou Ali askest of me now.
ALI	I ask thee to explain what thou hast said About thy husband.
WAJDAH	That's the riddle I Now bring to thee, for thou alone canst solve it.
ALI	(Rising in anger) And durst thou mock us, woman?
WAJDAH	(In a placating tone) Nay, Ali; The lashes can not rise above the brow.
ALI	But they can fall to shield the eye of treason.
WAJDAH	Would I could pluck it out for thine own sake.
ALI	Cajole[1] us not; for if that furtive eye Looks not upon us now, it looks on thee, Even every day.
WAJDAH	And wouldst thou thus impeach The faithfulness and loyalty of Wajdah?
ALI	When our friend Wajdah plots against our State---
WAJDAH	(Sharply) I meddle not in the affairs of the State.

---

1. To persuade by flattery or promises.

ALI	Thy husband and thy son?
WAJDAH	I swear to thee, I have nor son, nor husband.
ALI	Woman, beware!
WAJDAH	Believe me, Ali, for I speak the truth; I lost my husband many years ago, And until now I have not found my son!
ALI	But Mustafa and Kice--
WAJDAH	(In an inflection of painful memory) They were thy choice For me as son and husband, were they not?
ALI	But are they not? Is not Kice thine own son?
WAJDAH	That is what I would know of the Imam;-- That is the riddle which I beg of thee To solve for Wajdah, for thy loyal friend. Upon thine own persuasion I accepted Mustafa as husband--that is true-- But only on condition, thou'lt recall, That the boy he brought with him was my own son. If Kice is not my son, Then, Mustafa is not my husband.
ALI	(In a pensive manner) That In sooth would follow, but--
WAJDAH	Is Kice my son? Didst not Mustafa lie to thee, to me, And to thy wife to gain his wicked end?
ALI	In conscience, that is too much to presume.-- But we are drifting from the purpose now. I sent for thee to ascertain the truth--

41

WAJDAH	When I was coming of my own accord To tell thee that my wealth, my name, my life, Are in the hand of treason, Which, to my sorrow, harbors in my house.
ALI	Allah and the Prophet! Thou art true. But why dist thou not thus confess at first?
WAJDAH	Because thou didst not welcome me as friend,-- Because thou didst offend the loyal Wajdah With thy suspicions.--Now, that I have told thee, O valiant friend of truth, where treason harbors, Wilt thou not tell me what thou know'st of Kice?
ALI	Only that he's thy son.
WAJDAH	But that I doubt.
ALI	And I can not uphold thee in thy doubt Unless I doubt the story of Mustafa.
WAJDAH	But tell me, billah, didst thou then believe it?
ALI	I did.
WAJDAH	And dost thou still?
ALI	I have no cause To doubt now what I once believed.
WAJDAH	(Throwing up her hands) Alas! That he who is vicegerent of the Prophet,-- He who by virtue of this holy office Is nearest to the fountain-head of truth And prescience and infallibility, Should be deceived, and as deceivable As they the godless of the nomad kind, Even as I a wretched pagan woman. I came to thee for help; but thou dost seem,

Despite thy kinsman's claim to revelation,
As helpless as myself. Farewell, Ali--
And farewell to they Prophet and thy god!

(Exit)

ALI   Dispelled the clouds of doubt and hesitation.
Her wealth, her name, her life are in the hands
Of treason--treason harbors in her house--
And to her sorrow--We shall reave thee, friend,
Of all thy sorrows. Ahmed, come, and Kleib.
Orders for the arrest
Of Mustafa and Kice;
Anon, but with the least ado and coil.
Secretly and quietly, lest those
Who follow them blow in the smothered fire.
And in our absence no one here should know
That they are in the prison. Understand?
Elsewise you will be called upon, and oft,
To quell sedition. Come.

AHMED   (Aside) O Mustafa,
No longer shalt thou darken Ahmed's way:
Thy day was my night, thy night is now my day.

(Exeunt)

ACT II

Scene I

A GARDEN in front of WAJDAH's house on the bank of the river Euphrates. House with (practicable) door. Part of the garden wall with open gate. A clay bench under the palm trees. Bronze lamps hanging from branches and in front of the door. A lighted fire in a brazier near which are coffee utensils and coffee cups on a brass tray. Two square pillars about five feet in height, made of rough stone; one near the clay bench, the other in the centre of the stage, on which are brass cressets holding live coals. On the river bank across, the desert and palm groves in perspective.

Evening: full moon.

ZEID discovered near the brazier, pulverizing coffee in a wooden mortar; and Mahmoud spreading rugs and cushions on the clay bench and in front of it. Enter SALWAH.

SALWAH   The lamps not lit, the incense not yet burning?
            Leave off, Mahmoud; call thou Labibah here.---
            And bring with thee the myrrh and frankincense.

            (Exit Mahmoud.)

            These loutish slaves!

            (Resets the cushions)

            These Ethiopean clowns!

            (Enter LABIBAH)

LABIBAH   What is it!

SALWAH   Light the lamps.

LABIBAH   On such an evening?

SALWAH   Aye, and ask no questions.--(To herself) Light for sorrow!

45

(Labibah with a taper lights the oil lamps in the bronze cases.)

(Re-enter MAHMOUD bringing incense on a tray; Salwah places a little of the contents of the bowl in the cressets.)

And yet, this seems a mockery; the moon
On such a night makes light of our desire.
There--(Feeding the last cresset)
Now, go fill thy lap with lemon blossoms
And pomegranate flowers.--(To herself) Flowers for sorrow!

(Exit MAHMOUD)

Labibah, bring the tabor and the reeds.

(Exit LABIBAH)

An evening this, when even the moonlit sails
Upon the river undulate with song.
But Wajdah, why is she so sad these days,
When old Mustafa seldom shows his face!
For ever since those muffled beduins ceased
To prowl about the garden in the night,
We saw him not. But I am glad they're gone
Their secret business to conduct elsewhere.

(Enter WAJDAH)

I'm glad to see thee early out this evening.

WAJDAH   Early or late, it is the same, Salwah.

SALWAH   O, say not that.

WAJDAH   What wilt thou have me say?

SALWAH   On such an evening--

WAJDAH   I should fill my heart,
If it were vacant as the heart of Zeid,
With flowers of love and music. I would not
Thus wear the crown of sorrow and disdain
These silver coins of joy the generous moon

Strews on the clapping branches of the palms.
Oh, mother o'me! (Throws herself on the divan)
Is not the coffee ready?

SALWAH   In a trice.
A dance the while?
(Wajdah shrugs her shoulders)
No? Yes; I'll dance to-night.

(Salwah claps her hands; four or five slave-girls enter and stand in a line up stage, while she, with a veil in her hand, and Mahmoud, with the reeds, dance around the incense- bearing column in the centre; one of the slave-girls plays the rebab, and Zeid, with rhythmic accompaniment, pounds the coffee in the wooden mortar. After Salwah had executed the veil dance, she turns her step towards the slave-girls, who immediately take up the cue and dance down stage, and then around the column with her. While this dance is at its height, the distant voice of the Muazzen, calling the Faithful to the evening prayer, is heard.)

Allahu akbar, Allahu akbar!
La ilah illallah, la ilaha illallah!

(The dance stops abruptly, and the girls, except Salwah, go to their quarters to perform their devotion. Mahmoud and Zeid and Salwah kneel for a moment under the palms. Wajdah remains seated on the divan.)

WAJDAH   The call that conquered once my soul! But now,
It does not stir an atom of my being.

SALWAH   (Rising and coming towards her) Why art thou sad?

WAJDAH   Aye, why? The scented breeze
On such an evening melts the heaviest grief
And makes it flow a murmuring stream of joy.

SALWAH   Why art thou then so sad?

WAJDAH	(Somewhat perplexed) My disposition.
SALWAH	Thy disposition never seemed beyond The reach of solace, as it is this evening.
WAJDAH	Solace? If I but knew it could be found Somewhere, and were it far as yonder stars, Here would I lay me down and wait until The cycle of my destiny 's complete, Even as I waited, silent and resigned, These many years. But where is solace, Salwah, to be found? Where is my son,--my god--my father's kingdom? The dream I had last night Would make the ruined castle and the temple, In which my body and my soul were reared, Seem like a flaming pit, That hungers for my body and my soul.-- I ask myself, is this then what Islam Has promised me, --is this its gift divine? A dungeon for a kingdom, and a chain For all the gold and silver I have poured Into the coffers of the Prophet's heirs? For am I but a prisoner in this house? A slave, indeed, to this detested dotard, Who now spends the remainder of my fortune Among the rebels? (Mahmoud serves the coffee)
SALWAH	Tell me of thy dream.
WAJDAH	Kice is my son, they say, and so said I; But last night some one said that he is not. I dreamt that a phoenix came into this garden, Carrying upon his wings a comely youth With curled locks, high brow and dark brown eyes. It wakened me with whispers in my ear: "Behold thy son, O Wajdah, this thy son." I looked; and there, where thou art standing now,

He stood and smiled a melancholy smile
That should evoke the glory of my past.
"My son, my son" exclaiming, I rush forth;
But there I fell, alas! beneath that palm,
With nothing but a shadow in mine eyes,
And nothing but the dust upon my lips.

SALWAH   Is Kice not then thy son?

WAJDAH   (Reprovingly) Thou wouldst know all:

SALWAH   Hast thou not always with they confidence
            Honored me, and have I ever betrayed it?
            Then, why withhold it from me now?

WAJDAH   Invoke
            Thy fancy then: behold, a towered castle
            Upon the summit of a wooded hill
            O'erlooking two deep valleys;--one is called
            The valley of lions,
            The other is the valley of deers.
            Now, in that castle lived a pagan maid,
            The daughter, of the mighty al-Khattaf
            Who ruled the Yemen to the sea. She was called
            The princess of the women of the tribes.
            That pagan lass, the daughter of fair fortune,
            As wild and lithe and fair as the gazelles
            Of her fair hills, as graceful as their flowers,
            And as intrepid as their lions, too,
            Could wield the bow and javelin as but few
            Hunters and warriors could.
            Happy in her sports was she,
            And happier, in sooth, among her flowers.
            The limpid southern sky was, as it were,
            Warmed by the sun of her undying smile;
            And all the rippling rivulets and streams
            Ran down the valleys echoing her laughter.
            Alas! if Time on such suspicious days

49

Would stop to take a rest, and, resting, sleep
Only to rise when we would rest from joy.

SALWAH   And what befell her?

WAJDAH   Yes, I will continue.
           With bow in hand and quiver on her shoulder,
           She and her brother in the early dawn
           Set out one day upon the hunt.
           And by a chance, among the hunters rare,
           The arrows of another and her own
           One gazelle struck; and straightway he appeared,
           A youth beyond compare,
           To claim the victim of his bow.
           But when they met, the huntsman and the maid,
           Around the fallen, bleeding deer, their eyes
           Sought in each other what no prey can give,
           And gave each other--well, the gods decree.
           Soon after, yes, in wedlock they were bound;
           And in the following spring the bridal bed
           Was richer with the living fruit of love.
           That bride, O Salwah 's I; the child is mine.

SALWAH   And dist thou not bring him with thee to Koufah?

WAJDAH   No, I did not; for in that woeful year,
           When my first child, my only child was born,
           The kingdom of my father was invaded
           By Ali and the forces of Islam.
           Battalions of my father's army, one
           After the other, rushed against the hordes;
           But those who were not conquered by the cry
           That Allah 's one, were conquered by the sword,
           And none came back to tell the sorry tale.
           My husband, then, marched out against Ali
           Leading my father's guards.
           And when I looked out of the castle tower
           To wave my sleeve, my child was at my breast.
           Dread day and darkest night of anguish! They

50

Were followed by a darker morning when
The cry of Islam and of Ali's hounds
Convulsed the castle walls.
I rushed to the tower, and in that rolling sea
Of glistening arms, what dost thou think I saw?
O lack-a-day, I cried, O woeful sight!
My blood was aflame--it hissed within my veins;
It crackled in my heart; it blazed in my eyes;--
I forgot my child.
And in that sea of horror I could see
Only my husband's head upon a spear.
Revenge, revenge! The voice that cried
Was heard above the tumult--it was mine.
I dunned my mail and flew into the saddle;
I spurred my horse, and, flashing through the ranks,
Called out to Ali son of Abi-Taleb,
"Come, meet a woman now in single combat!"
Young Ali forward came; but I was mad.--
Could I my valor match with his? could I
At least resist the magic of his words,
Which he intoned in strains miraculous?
Yes, I was conquered, not by Ali's arm,
Not by his prowess and superior strength,
But by the sound of words from Allah's book,
As it is called,--of words that seemed divine
When I first heard them. I--I was disarmed.
And though a captive, I began to feel
The beauty and the freedom of a faith
That sang itself into Arabia's heart.
Allahu akbar! I too often cried;
But now these words, and though they fall from high
Like music thrice a day upon my ear,
Remind me only that I'm thrice accursed.

SALWAH   But what befell thy child?

WAJDAH   (Putting incense in the cresset) My child? alas!

51

(Enter KICE Wajdah is startled when she hears footsteps at the gate)

KICE

Peace with thee, mother.

WAJDAH

(Overcoming her agitation) And with thee sweetest peace.

(Exit Salwah)

Why comest late, O Kice?

KICE

(Oblivious of everything but the uprising against Ali and the war)
I was detained
By some of our true friends. But Koufah now
Is arming; for the war has been declared,
The armorers are reconciled, and all--

WAJDAH

Of what import is that to us, O Kice?
We soon shall be in Yemen and away
From all these intrigues, these consuming fires?
Are we not going to the Yemen, Kice?

KICE

Kice can not long remain where thou art not.

(Wajdah kisses him)

(Enter MAHMOUD with his lap full of flowers, which he strews on the divan and curtsying, withdraws.)

WAJDAH

These flowers transport me to the happy land
That calls us, never ceasing, to her heart.
Here is the fragrance of my native gardens;
Here is the beauty of my native hills;
And in this flower (taking up a pomegranate blossom)

The warmth of Yemen skies.

(Aside) A burning memory in it, too, for in
The pomegranate season he was born.
(To Kice) Dost thou not like the pomegranate flowers?
These fallen kisses from the lips of love,--

52

These vases moulded of the sighs of love,--
These crimson cups filled with the wine of love.
Ah, see, they are as red as thine own lips.

(Kisses him in the mouth)

Thou dost seem tired.

KICE   I am; and yet I must
                Be out again; I must rejoin my friends.

WAJDAH   To-night? No, no.

KICE   (Going toward the house) Even now.

WAJDAH   (Following him) It can not be.
                Thou must not venture out again to-night.

KICE   My friends await outside--there's yet a chance--
                And there's no danger--be assured, O mother.
                Nor will I be out long.

                (Exit)

WAJDAH   And can it be, O Heaven! can it be?
                Why this unholy craving, if it be?
                Am I a mother? God, wherefore this love?
                Am I a mother? Why the lurid flame
                Within this breast, if on this breast he leaned
                His infant head--if from this breast....
                O Almanee, O god of mine own father,
                Before whose altar I have burned this myrrh,
                Thee I invoke, to thee I turn for light.
                O guide me, free me from the slaying thralls   束缚
                Of this deep mystery.
                Say, if it be my son upon whose eyes
                I dare to fix the sickly gaze of passion;
                Say, if it be my son upon whose lips
                I leave the foul contagion of my soul;
                Say, if it be my son whom I would drag

With me into the seething pits of hell.
Wajdah calls to thee, O Almanee!
Wajdah comes to thee again for light.
O, guide her now that she might find her son,--
That she might know her son.

(Drop)

Scene II

A Street in Koufah. Drums heard in the distance, and people within shouting, Allah! Allah!

Enter TABTABA.

TABTABA   A miracle is man!
For he can fight--and pray.
Allah, Allah!
And then he drinks his brother's blood.
The wolf can not do that.
But that is why he's not a man:
He can not stand on his hind legs and pray.
A miracle indeed is man!
For he can steal--and pray.
Allah! Allah!
And then he steals his neighbor's wife.
The lion can not do that.
But that is why he's but a lion:
He can not stand on his hind legs and pray.

(Enter SHEIBAN carrying a shield and a few swords and spears under his arms).

And here comes one who's neither wolf nor lion.

SHEIBAN   Salaam, O Tabtaba.

TABTABA   Salaam, Sheiban.
How fares it with thee now?
Didst thou get any silver for the shouting?

SHEIBAN	Indeed I did, and more than I deserve-- Allah be praised.
TABTABA	For making men of brass. But tell me art thou going to the war?
SHEIBAN	Ah, no; I have a conscience; I do not Believe in shedding blood.
TABTABA	(Aside) Nor wolf nor lion Is he, nor even a man. (To Sheiban) But canst thou make A weapon for thy conscience? Or dost have A conscience only during war?
SHEIBAN	I have--
TABTABA	A skillful conscience to make weapons, eigh?
SHEIBAN	We are commanded--
TABTABA	Happy to obey!
SHEIBAN	And why not, when a rusty piece of brass, Which we fit to a bamboo stick, will bring Full ten pieces of silver?
TABTABA	Shrewd Sheiban! But Allah will melt thy silver and gold? And pour it moulten hot into thy throat, If thou dost not enlist in the **jehad**.
SHEIBAN	Is't not enough that we the weapons make? How could the Faithful fight, wilt tell me that, If we did not sit in our shops And hammer at our steel? Aye, he hath fought his fight who even blows The armorer's fire.... Look at this shield;--my heart is in it. Aye,

And when it goes to battle, I am there,
I mean herein. (Pointing to the shield)

TABTABA   Herein I find thee mean,
And meaningless, and cowardly, and false.
Who can not wield a weapon or would not--

SHEIBAN   But I can make one.

TABTABA   Thou art even rude
To interrupt me thy superior. Hear
What I would say:
Who would not wield a weapon is not worth
To Arabia the dropping of a camel!

SHEIBAN   (Turning to go away) Not even if his purse is full of gold?
I thank thee, Tabtaba.

TABTABA   Be thou convinced
Before thou thankest me. Consider this:
If Koufah was attacked by Allah's foes,
Couldst thou with all thine arms defend thyself?

SHEIBAN   Not with my arms perhaps, but with my legs.
But thou couldst not with either arms or legs.
Now canst thou run?--ha, ha, ha!--run away?

(Sheiban runs out, but Tabtaba follows him and drags him
back by the cloak.)

TABTABA   I run away? thou foul breath of a hag?
I say, thou art not worth a camel's dropping.
I run away? Give me that shield.

(Snatches the shield and a sword from him.)

Behold!
This is the Tabtaba of years ago
When thus he stood and shook his mortal blade.
Alas, alas!

That was when in this breast the martial fire
Incessant flamed; when in these torpid veins
The boiling blood wrought marvels in the fight;
When in these ears the din and shock of steel
Were sweetest music; when the dust and smoke
Of battle were dawn-like in mine eyes;
And when the smell of blood--have at thee, churl!
Thy stand! for though I smell no blood in thee,
I'll tutor thee, for Allah's sake, in combat.

(Executes a few flourishes.)

Be not afraid.

(In assuring and mocking tone.)

SHEIBAN   (With questioning trepidation.) Thou art in earnest then?

TABTABA   (Practicing a feint) This for they heart, but lo, it's on thy head.
               Defend thy guts this time,--but hast thou any?
               Eigh! what's the use? I'm labeling thy steel--
               Debasing it for what? A camel's dropping!--
               But I must now begone.
               I must find Kice, else Wajdah will go mad.
               Hast thou seen Kice to-day?

SHEIBAN   No, I have not.

TABTABA   Nor heard about him.

SHEIBAN   Yes, I heard it said
               That, with the rebels who escaped, he's gone
               To join Moawia's army.

TABTABA   Life of Allah!
               No happy tidings this, for Wajdah, no.
               I hope it is not true.

               (Exit)

57

SHEIBAN	(Running after him) Ho, Tabtaba! Come back; give me my sword and shield.
	(Re-enter TABTABA, and taking some coins out of his pocket, throws them contemptuously to Sheiban.)
TABTABA	Take this--some silver--for thy shield and sword.
	(Exit)
SHEIBAN	(Picking up the coins.) What a rich poet! Would I could I make rhymes Instead of spears. But he would not be rich, I trow, If he was not a water carrier too.
	(Slow curtain while he is still picking up the coins.)

Scene III

A Room in WAJDAH's House, furnished with carpets, big square cushions and leaning pillows, and one divan.

WAJDAH and SALWAH discovered; SALWAH kneeling on a cushion near the divan, chafing Wajdah's hands.

WAJDAH	What happiness one finds in but a breath, When death's the giver.
SALWAH	Art thou better now?
WAJDAH	A little; but I would feel better still If we were now upon our dromedaries Out in the open desert.
SALWAH	Very soon, If it pleases Allah.
WAJDAH	If it pleases Allah? Ah, well--but has not Tabtaba returned?

SALWAH	Not yet.
WAJDAH	O Kice!--I should not have allowed Him yesternight to venture out at all. Forebodings, like a tiger's claws, Dig in my breast.
SALWAH	But Mahmoud has come back Bringing with him a sheaf from rumor's field. Shall I tell thee?
WAJDAH	Tell me, tell me all.
SALWAH	Mustafa, 'tis said, was put to death For treason.
WAJDAH	(In an accent of surprise, followed by an inflection of irony.) Eigh! That is too bad, too bad. But greater men have died a meaner death.-- And where is Kice?
SALWAH	Nothing is said of Kice.
WAJDAH	Oh. mother o'me! And what about the war?
SALWAH	The Khalif and his forces have set out Against the enemy.
WAJDAH	But Kice, where's Kice? (She rises from the divan and paces worried across the room.)
SALWAH	He'll soon be here with Tabtaba, I hope. But shall I give thee more of what is blown By idle rumor, though unwillingly I make my tongue the bearer?
WAJDAH	Speak.

SALWAH	They say That thou hast openly renounced--
WAJDAH	My faith? the faith of Islam? That is true.
SALWAH	And that thou art espied by Ali's friends.
WAJDAH	She of the house-top need not be espied. (Hesitatingly)
SALWAH	And that thou lovest thine own son,-- (Unconsciously defiant)
WAJDAH	Where be the mother that loves not her son?
SALWAH	(After a moment's silence) But, Princess Wajdah--
WAJDAH	(Ruefully) Yes, I know thy drift. O, that the gods would not reveal the truth About it all.
SALWAH	Then Kice is not they son?
WAJDAH	Who knows but the accursed Mustafa? Yet might there not be found in all the world Another one this sad knot to untie? If I but knew my mother were alive, Or any other servants of the castle I left behind me on that fatal day;-- If I but knew that Gannam lived somewhere, I would not cease to wander and inquire Throughout the wide and lone land of the Arabs Until I found him.
SALWAH	Gannam?
WAJDAH	Or my mother, Or some one that could give my soul relief.

SALWAH	But why doubt now that Kice is thine own son?
WAJDAH	Because the soul is not deceived forever,-- Because a mother ought to know her son, And thou the gods should pluck him from her breast A puling babe, and after many years Should guide him back to her a bearded man.
SALWAH	Forgive me, Princess Wajdah, if I ask More questions than I ought. But Mustafa, Why did he thee deceive?
WAJDAH	And Why do men Wear swords and trim their beards, when in their hearts Is neither bravery nor aught of grace?-- No truth of what the manner would proclaim? Because they are the slaves Of their own little selves, and not the slaves Of love, when they would gain the love of woman.
	(Enter LABIBAH)
LABIBAH	Ahmed desires to see thee.
	(Wajdah motions to her to admit him. Exit Labibah.)
WAJDAH	(To Salwah) Send out Zeid To see why Tabtaba has not returned.
	(Exit Salwah)
	What can I say to Ahmed ere I know The truth?
	(Enter AHMED)
AHMED	Allah greet thee, Wajdah.
WAJDAH	And strengthen thee.
AHMED	And wed to fairer end this fair beginning.

61

WAJDAH	Nay--give us light to end this dark beginning.
AHMED	Why dark?
WAJDAH	Why fair?
AHMED	The end of suffering--
WAJDAH	But the beginning of the end is dark. Is not the false-dawn darker than the night?
AHMED	But we have done with that. Here is the sun (Pointing to his sword) That slew the night and false-dawn for thy sake.
WAJDAH	Then I am slain, for I am part of night.
AHMED	But from thine eyes a radiance ever flows.
WAJDAH	The more it flows the darker 't is within.
AHMED	No light in what I bring? (Approaching her)
WAJDAH	(Sitting on the divan) Light to the blind.
AHMED	Why so?
WAJDAH	What can she see whose soul is like--
AHMED	I hope thou dost not grieve for him.
WAJDAH	(Feigning ignorance) For whom?
AHMED	For him who was the source of all thy woe; For thy--but for thy sake I name him not.
WAJDAH	(Abstractedly) And didst thou slay him?
AHMED	No; the nation did.

WAJDAH	(Indifferently, but with an inflection of irony.) Why? Was he very dangerous?
AHMED	(Naively earnest) He was To thee, O Wajdah, if not to Islam.
WAJDAH	And what am I to Islam or to thee?
AHMED	To me, O Princess, thou art all Islam.
WAJDAH	But did I ever prompt thee to the deed?
AHMED	Thy love--I thought I read once in thine eyes; Thy love--I heard it whisper in my breast; They love--I saw it come with sword in hand.
WAJDAH	(Rising) But what about the nation and Islam?
AHMED	They were the judges, I the instrument Of execution.
WAJDAH	(In a semi-mocking tone) Executioner.
AHMED	(Mortified) O Princess Wajdah, play not on my words.
WAJDAH	(With a desire to prolong his visit till Kice returned.) Upon thy words, O Ahmed, not upon Thy meaning, which in sooth I can not grasp.
AHMED	Better in play than mockery, but both Would seem now out of place.
WAJDAH	What dost thou mean?
AHMED	Must I again retell thee what I mean? Must love forever languish thus unseen In melancholy longing? O, how long Will voiceless images and shadows throng My night of fear and doubt and sullen hope?

How long must love in barren darkness grope?
Or can it be that when two hearts are healed,
God gives to one a sword, to th'other a shield?
But I have need of none; at thy command,
I am a living weapon in thy hand.
Put me to service; use me as thou wilt;
Pluck out the precious gems that grace the hilt.
I am thy shield;--O press me to thy heart
And let magicians wonder at thine art!
For from my steel a silver stream will flow,
And on its banks the jasmine flower will blow.

WAJDAH   In such a stream my infant joy was drowned.

AHMED   Upon its banks thy joy shall spring again.

WAJDAH   No jasmine grows where noxious weeds abound.

AHMED   But where thou treadest no such weeds remain.
Aye, Wajdah, since thy shadow graced my dream,
My soul with pure and lofty thoughts did teem.
I heard thee whisper in my ear at night
Words to efface the most forbidding height.
And now I'm come thy freedom to enthrone
And crown with love, the purest ever known.
What sayst thou, Wajdah?

WAJDAH   Thou dost seek in vain
The God of thy dream in a ruined fane.
(Aside) What a resemblance!--This again the dream?

AHMED   But ruined temples more inspiring seem
Than those whose altars never see the sun
And around whom Time his magic never spun.
Yet, if thy fane were but a booth of hair,
Thy fate and fortune I would joy to share.
And though thou wander tentless in the land,
And though thy carpet be the burning sand,
Aye, billah, I am with thee everywhere,

For where so ever I worship, thou art there.
Speak--stab me not with silence, Wajdah--speak!

WAJDAH   The impossible, O Ahmed, thou dost seek.

AHMED   Not so; no so. How can it be that love
Is unkind on the earth, though kind above?
I feel that into this world I was beguiled,
And of thy love I suckled when a child.

WAJDAH   These amorous, mystic flowers are not for me.
(Aside) But can it be, O mother, can it be?

AHMED   For none but thee; I kiss the dust before thee.
And none but Ahmed, **billah**! shall adore thee.

WAJDAH   But why throw thus thy life into the tomb?
Why waste upon the waste thy scent and bloom?

AHMED   Without thee life is barren as the waste;
Without thee even Faith would bitter taste.

WAJDAH   But I'm a pagan now; I have renounced--

AHMED   I know; for that to Ali was announced.
To him it may be of import, not to me.
For though thou be as faithless as the sea,
As heartless as the desert, and as dire--
As cruel as the drudges of hell-fire,--
Aye, Wajdah, though thou creed less, godless be,
I still would follow and would worship thee.

WAJDAH   (Perturbed) Enough, enough--leave me--I am not well
(Aside) O god, these gathering, brooding clouds dispel.

AHMED   And wouldst thou have me leave thee thus?

WAJDAH	Aye, go. Leave me to my ignorance and woe.-- Speak not--go--stay. Hast thou seen Kice to-day.
AHMED	(Hesitating) NO.--But--Wajdah--
WAJDAH	Leave me now, I say. But come this evening.
AHMED	I shall come. Salaam. (Exit)
WAJDAH	I'll look upon them both, I'll question both. Too long has mystery gnawed[1] at my heart; Too long has sorrow fed upon this breast; Too long has spite piped on my broken soul; Too long has love--but soon I'll know the truth. And though my father's god hear not my prayer, I'll know the truth. Ahmed and Kice shall be My oracles;--I'll know the truth this evening. This very evening I shall have them both Before me in the garden, I shall know-- (Enter Tabtaba) At last! But why alone--where's Kice?
TABTABA	I questioned, searched, inquired everywhere, But not where Kice, might be.
WAJDAH	Why? where is he?
TABTABA	Not in the city, surely.
WAJDAH	(Impatient and anxious) Where, then, where?
TABTABA	He's gone to the war.

---

1. Troubled or tormented by constant annoyance.

WAJDAH	(Aghast) What sayest?
TABTABA	They all say. He's gone to join Moawia.
WAJDAH	Thou slave! The curse upon thee, bearer of ill tidings! Black face, call Mahmoud--nay, call Salwah--stay-- Call Ahmed back-- Tell him--no, no--no, no. (Sits down and ponders) What shall I do? Ahmed I can not see again Until I have seen Kice. Between the two I'm lost--forever lost-- Unless when I upon their faces look With love, the light of god, to guide my heart. Yes, yes; I'll look upon them both. I'll question both, and with an open mind.-- Have them prepare a tent, O Tabtaba, And saddle dromedaries. Go, be quick.

(Exit Tabtaba.)

I must seek him myself--I must seek Kice.

CURTAIN

ACT III

Scene I

THE DESERT.--A strong wind rising to a sand-storm as the scene develops.

Enter WAJDAH and TABTABA carrying a bow in his hand and an arrow-case swung across his shoulder.

TABTABA   (Covering his face up to his eyes with his kufeiyeh, or head-kerchief)
It is the Yemen wind, the harbinger
Of the simoom[1]--I know it by its voice.

WAJDAH   The Yemen wind is never so unkind,
So treacherous.

TABTABA   (Sniffing the air) And yet, I smell the south,
And feel the seering touch of southern gales.
See, there, the sand begins to whirl, to rise
In columns--shadows of the Jinn that dance
A welcome to Eblis.

WAJDAH   It matters not,
We must advance; the scene of battle now
Can not be far away.

TABTABA   But why not wait
Until the messenger returns? Mahmoud must be
By this time at Moawia's camp. Why then
Adventure forth before we know that Kice
Is with him? Hear the howling storm!
It is increasing, it is the simoom.

---

1. A hot, suffocating, sand laden wind of the deserts of Arabia.

WAJDAH   We'll wait therefore until Mahmoud returns.
             Go pitch the tent.

TABTABA   Thou hast forgotten, it seems,
             The desert etiquette when the simoom
             Is her guest. We must bow, prostrate ourselves;
             And as for tents and pegs--I'll dig a hole,
             O Wajdah, for my head. But rest thee here
             Among these clumps; I'll find a refuge yonder.

             (Exit Tabtaba)

WAJDAH   The desert guest shall find me seated. Yes,
             I'll sit upon this rock and wait. The storms
             Of fortune I withstood for many years;--
             I can withstand the sand-storm for a day.

             (The storm continues, increasing in volume.)

             Blow on, blow on, ye howling fiends of hell,
             Ye myriad-mouthed goblins of the gale,
             Ye dusky hissing serpents of the waste,
             Ye afrits of the all-consuming sands.
             But bring back my beloved Kice, and blow
             Until you seer me like an autumn leaf;
             O, bring back my beloved Kice, and blow
             Until you make of me a column of sand;
             O, bring back my beloved Kice, and blow
             Until there be of Wajdah but a breath;--
             But bring him back before I lose my sight--
             Oh, wouldst tattoo my face?

             (She covers her face with her veil and turns her head away
             from the wind, as she rises to seek a shelter.)
             (Re-enter TABTABA)

TABTABA   O Princess Wajdah,
             I see approaching us a cloud of dust--
             It must be Mahmoud.

WAJDAH   Where!

TABTABA	Look, look.
WAJDAH	I see; But I can not distinguish yet--
TABTABA	Two riders, two.
WAJDAH	I see but one.
TABTABA	(Scanning the horizon) Two, billah! I see two.
WAJDAH	Get in the saddle--gallop forth and meet them (Exit Tabtaba) I see but one: Mahmoud is come alone. Yet I have left some strength to hear the worst.-- Eigh, dead? he fell in battle, dost thou say? Oh, Oh! But I have dreamt again the very dream: Last night he also came into the garden Riding upon a phoenix like a chief Returning from the war a conqueror.-- (Re-enter TABTABA with a disappointed look.)
TABTABA	It's not Mahmoud.
WAJDAH	Who then?
TABTABA	A stranger who Is on his way to Koufah to see Wajdah.
WAJDAH	To see me? Who is he?
TABTABA	I can not say. He's muffled; and he would not give his name.
WAJDAH	A stranger! muffled!--there's no harm in that. Yet, might there not be good? Go call him here.

(Tabtaba goes and motions to the stranger)

'O joy, if what I now foresee is true!
If not,--whoever he be, whatever he brings,
I welcome all: I am prepared to hear
The blackest messenger from deepest hell.

(Enter Gannam)

But often in adversity the light
Comes sooner from a stranger than a friend.

GANNAM   Peace on thee, Princess Wajdah.

WAJDAH   And on thee, peace.
Who be the Arab?

GANNAM   One whom Wajdah knows.

WAJDAH   Eigh, but whence comest?

GANNAM   From the South.

WAJDAH   What part?

GANNAM   The Yemen.

WAJDAH   Of what tribe?

GANNAM   Of Kahtan, I.

WAJDAH   (Anxious) And of what branch?

GANNAM   Of Tye.

WAJDAH   What house?

GANNAM   Nubhan.

WAJDAH   (Moved) Then we--

GANNAM   (Uncovering his face) Nay, Princess, I am of their slaves.
            Dost thou remember not thy slave Gannam?

WAJDAH   Gannam! (She goes toward him overjoyed; he hastens to kiss
            her hand and she bends her head over his shoulder and kisses
            it.)

GANNAM   Even he, who kisses now thy hand.

WAJDAH   O mother o'me! how hast thou changed--thy hair--

GANNAM   The waves of Time and grief--enough of them
            To render hoary even the brows of babes.

WAJDAH   And what now brings thee to these climes?

GANNAM   The hope
            Of seeing thee again, and Kice.
            I learned that you were living yet in Koufah,
            And to my heart the news is such a balm
            That I would travel from the farthest parts
            Of Arabia---

WAJDAH   Who told thee of my son?

GANNAM   Even in Hedjaz and Yemen this is known.

WAJDAH   But dost thou not remember that my child,
            When I went out my husband to avenge,
            Was with my mother in the castle tower?

GANNAM   In very truth, I too was with them there.

WAJDAH   And was not the castle pillaged? 抢夺 抢夺

GANNAM   Aye, it was.

WAJDAH   And all the inmates slaughtered?

73

GANNAM   Most of them.
              Thy mother and thy child and I escaped.

WAJDAH   And what became of Kice and mother, say.

GANNAM   That were too sad a story now to tell;
              For I had never hoped to see thy son,
              And, in good truth, if we met now again,
              It were not possible to know each other.

WAJDAH   But tell me where went thou with mother and him
              After you had escaped; how long were you
              Together. Tell me all--and speak the truth.

GANNAM   When we escaped we never cherished hope
              Of ever seeing thee; we thought in sooth
              That thou wert gone to share thy husband's fate.
              And thus, with bitter sorrow in our hearts
              And nothing in our scrips, not even a crust,
              We wayfared to Oman; and among the booths
              Of Humyar Arabs found a welcome roof.
              We lived and wandered in those spicy climes
              For many years. But when thy mother--sad!
              Too sad it were to tell--
              The dew of Allah's mercy on her grave.
              But joyance might have lighted her last glance,
              And closed with tender hands her heavy lids,
              If she but knew that Kice was living still.

WAJDAH   Then Kice was lost before my mother died.

GANNAM   Be patient, Wajdah, I will tell thee all.
              One day--the fifth year had just touched his brow--
              He ran behind the camels in the field--
              He joyed to hold the udder at milking time--
              He'd carry singing to his grandam's tent
              A warm and foaming vessel of the milk--
              In those uncloudy yet unfriendly days,
              One Mustafa, a merchant from Hedjaz,

Crouched near our welcome booths his caravan.
He was our guest for many days;
His heart much leaned to Kice;
He coddled him and made him little presents
Of silks and spices from his camel-loads.
And when the day of his departure came,
He offered me a goodly sum for Kice.

WAJDAH   And thou didst sell him--thou didst sell my son?

GANNAM   Allah forfend!
Dearer to me than mine eyes was Kice.
But Mustafa said thus: I would adopt him;
I want a child to take my name and fortune.
Give him to me, and all these loads of silk
And musk and myrrh and ambergris, are thine.

WAJDAH   And thou wert tempted--Allah pardon thee.

GANNAM   No, by an Arab's troth! But fearing what
I thought in Mustafa an evil eye,
We straightway westward moved; we came to Teyma.
But even in that verdant land, ill-fortune,
A few years after, hovered o'er our tents
And carried Kice away.
How, and wherefore, and whereto, we knew not.

WAJDAH   Then Kice was but a boy when he was lost.

GANNAM   In sooth.

WAJDAH   And canst thou recognize him now.

GANNAM   Not if we chanced to meet upon the road.

WAJDAH   And canst thou under any circumstance?

GANNAM   In sooth, I can

WAJDAH	And how?
GANNAM	Call him; and I Will tell thee in a trice if he's thy son.
WAJDAH	But how couldst thou assure thyself and me?
GANNAM	By a simple sign--a mark upon his arm.
WAJDHA	A simple sign, what sign?
GANNAM	Upon his arm There is tattooed beneath a prominent mole A simulacrum of the amulet Which thou thyself didst hang around his neck.
WAJDAH	(Ruminating) A simulacrum of the amulet?-- Yes, yes; I now remember. O, for joy! The secret I'll unlock; I have the key. But--might I ever find the door again?
TABTABA	(Who had been looking out) Mahmoud is come.-- (Shaking his head ruefully) Alas, alone.
WAJDAH	(Dumbfounded) Alone! Enter MAHMOUD, bows, and presents a message. Wajdah reads it and as for a moment, as if stunned by a heavy blow, rigid and dumb; the message falls from her hands. She cries, beating her breast, and falls near the rock weeping.

Scene II

Open Court in WAJDAH's House. A fountain in the centre, and all around a low portico with lamps hanging from the ceiling; straw shades rolled up on one side and half-drawn on the other to keep out the sun. Two clay benches on both sides of the fountain, on one of which are a rebab and a tray of lemon and pomegranate blossoms. Entrances.

76

Time: afternoon.

SALWAH and LABIBAH discovered.

LABIBAH   And why would she leave Koufah!

SALWAH   To save her life.

LABIBAH   But what is her offence?

SALWAH   Poor innocent!
             Dost know not that she has renounced her faith?

LABIBAH   But the Khalif is her friend.

SALWAH   And though he be,
             He can not to the people shut his ear.

LABIBAH   And what of Kice, what does the message say?

SALWAH   Moawia says that he had heard that Kice
             Had come to join his forces, but--

LABIBAH   But what?

SALWAH   They searched, and could not find him in the ranks.

LABIBAH   And did he fall in battle?

SALWAH   Allah knows.

LABIBAH   Poor Mistress Wajdah! Where will she now go?

SALWAH   I know not. Ask me not another question.

LABIBAH   One more, I beg. Must we not go with her?

SALWAH   What though we must.

77

LABIBAH	But I would know thy mind.
SALWAH	Only death shall sever me from Wajdah.
LABIBAH	I too will go with her.
	(Enter WAJDAH)
WAJDAH	Labibah, Salwah--
	My sisters, not my slaves--now fare ye well.
SALWAH	I have no heart to utter or to hear
	The words of parting.
	Thy leal and loving slave will go with thee.
WAJDAH	What would you have with me, what would you share,
	That I am now an outcast at whose heel
	The dogs of fanaticism yelp and bark,--
	Even the empty spaces scowl and yawn.
SALWAH	Nothing that ease and affluence can give;
	For I should be the happiest of slaves,
	If in the desolation of thy let,
	Thou wouldst yet deem me indispensible.
LABIBAH	Aye, Princess Wajdah, we would serve thee still;
	For if the Arabs banish thee from Koufah,
	They can not banish thee from us, thy slaves.
WAJDAH	May he who rules our fate requite you love.
	Where is Mahmoud?
SALWAH	He's here.
WAJDAH	And Tabtaba?
SALWAH	Is gone for water.

| WAJDAH | (To Labibah) Send Mahmoud at once |
| | For Ahmed. Say, I want to see him now. |

(Exit Labibah)

Thou Salwah, thou art mistress of this house;
Be kind to all, and Tabtaba 'bove all.
This parchment thou wilt keep secure with thee.
(Handing a scroll)
And if some friendly stranger to my fate
Come to inquire about me, say thou this:
Wajdah is gone to breathe the desert air.--
And might I not, O Salwah, ever chance
To meet thee in my wanderings? And what
If thou be then the Mistress, and I be--
But thou'lt be kinder to me, wilt thou not,
Than I have been to thee? Weep not, my friend;
For fortune, ever changing like the moon,
Can never set on any one's domain,
Without it rise anon upon another's.

| SALWAH | Such fortune as would raise me above Wajdah |
| | And cut me off from her, I would not have. |

WAJDAH	Thou art as good and brave as thou art foolish.
	But in such trials as are now reserved
	For me betwixt the desert and the grave,
	I should ill-minded be if tender plants
	I took with me into the wilderness.
	Remain thou here; thy heart shall flower joy
	In freedom's garden, 'neath thy rising star.

| SALWAH | Why wilt thou not appeal to the Imam? |

WAJDAH	There's naught that he can do, for I am now
	Sole mistress of my fate; and I believe
	That with the nomads of the wilderness
	More human good and solace will I find.
	Aye, Wajdah 'll be a beduin woman now,
	As liegeless as she was in her own hills,

In Yemen, and as free as she was born.
Better the desert sands than city Arabs;
Better the desert sun than city splendor.
But woe in me one thing will ever gnaw
Into my heart, and though beyond the sea
And to the farthest end of savage land
Myself I banish: I can forget all,
Once to the wilderness I turn my face;
For neither past nor present ever rule
From grave or throne the fate of nomad kind;--
All but this smiting mystery and Kice,
All but my son and sin, I can forget.
That once I was the darling flower of dales
Where lions prowl and nimble gazelles amble,
I can forget; that with an evil hand
My father's throne and temple I destroyed,
I can forget; that I have turned against
My kinsmen and my clan, I can forget;
That I have fought with Ali side by side
Against my father for a doting faith,
I can forget; that I have given my wealth
To further a religion that degrades
And fetters woman, makes of her a slave,
I can forget; that I myself have lived
In bondage, dallying for many years
On cushions under which the vipers curl,
I can forget; but that I now might be
A mother like whom, since the days of Aad,
No other mother was or ever shall be,--
O gods of heaven! how can I this forget?

(Enter TABTABA)

TABTABA   Thy life is now in danger, Princess Wajdah.
            The incensed Arabs clamor for thy blood,--
            They call thee infidel and traitor and
            Apostate and a pagan dog!--Be quick,
            Be quick! Let us depart--let's hence in haste.

            (Enter LABIBA, MAHMOUD and ZEID)

WAJDAH	I'd let them slay me, if their hands were clean To offer sacrifice.
TABTABA	We must not tarry.
WAJDAH	'T is thus set down. Remember me, my friends, When in the silk robes of a better lot You might have slaves yourselves to do your will. For I do now requite you all with freedom. And Tabtaba, see thou that my live wealth Is equally divided as set down In what I gave to Salwah.
TABTABA	Billah, no; For I go with thee.
WAJDAH	Nay, I go alone.
TABTABA	Life of this day, thou shalt not go alone. For who but Tabtaba shall sing to thee Of water and thy water-carrier be?
WAJDAH	I go alone.
TABTABA	But am I not Free now To follow thee if so I list? Nay, billah, nay; I tarry not behind. Thou shalt not, Wajdah, nomadize alone.
WAJDAH	And canst thou suffer long the nomad life?
TABTABA	And does a princess ask a beduin that? Withal a poet? Aye, and I was born Within the desert, salted in the sands, Was suckled at the breast of nomad life, And ever do I harp and rhyme upon This nomad life? Nay, by the Prophet's beard!--
WAJDAH	Saddle my favorite dromedary--go.

TABTABA	O, that it were thy fate!
	How I would saddle and muzzle it for thee.

(Exit)

WAJDAH	And ye, my loving friends, straightway prepare
	A set-out for the wayfare; I would not
	Be cumbered with much stuff and futile gear:
	Only a poke of dates, a water skin,
	And coverings the chill of night requires.

(Exeunt Servants)

(The voice of the Muazzen, calling the Faithful to the afternoon prayer, is heard in the distance.)

Allahu akbar, allahu akbar!
La ilaha illallah, la ilaha illallah!

(Wajdah of a sudden covers her ears with her hands and goes to the divan and sits down, exasperated, impatient for the agony to pass.)

WAJDAH	No more, O blind Muazzen, will thy voice
	Like daggers fall upon a bleeding heart;
	No more will it a memory evoke
	That licks my suffering with a tongue of flame:--
	Farewell to thy Mohammed and thy Faith,
	Farewell to Koufah. And to ye, farewell,
	O prison-walls of destiny, O walls
	Of crumbling cruelty and servitude!
	Within your shades to bondage I was wooed;
	Within your shades to freedom I aspired,
	And dreamed of things that mortals can not grasp.
	Farewell, O flowers of iridescent dreams,

(Taking the flowers from the tray and strewing them on the ground.)

Farewell, O dreams of pomegranate flowers.
O love wrapped in the mystery of pain,
O mystery of bitter bliss, farewell.--
But if he be not dead--if he yet live--

Might not the desert give him back to me?
Alas! I'm ever thus the sport of fate;
For when Gannam is sent to me with the sign
That clears or criminates my smitten heart,
Death overtakes the shade of sudden joy
And buries it forever in the sands.--
No, not forever! We shall meet again--
And that not far.
And I shall recognize thee better then,--
Shall know thee better, yea, and better love thee.

(Takes up the rebab and sings plaintively.)

SONG

Within the groves of paradise,
Where milk and honey streams meander,
With us, in fairest nomad guise,
    The sultana of song shall wander.
And everywhere the honey glance of flowers
Shall call us to the love-feast in their bowers;
    For there
Joy never ends, love never dies:
    How sweet to rove, my Fair,
Beneath the palms of paradise.

And luminous clouds of every hue--
    Of saffron soft and crimson red,
Of brightest gold and fairest blue--
    Shall veil, conceal our rosy bed;
And fairy forms immortal in our sky
    Shall whisper "Peace!" as they are flitting by;
    For there
Joy never ends, love never dies:
    How sweet to dream, my Fair,
Beneath the palms of paradise.

(Enter GANNAM hurriedly, interrupting the Song towards
the end.)

GANNAM   O Wajdah, happy tidings!

WAJDAH	(Rising, startled) Thou Gannam?
GANNAM	I bring thee happy tidings--Kice is here-- In Koufah.
WAJDAH	(Stunned) Eigh! Repeat thy words
GANNAM	In sooth, Kice is in Koufah still.
WAJDAH	Kice living!
GANNAM	Yes; But he's in prison.
WAJDAH	(Rushes towards him) Do I hear thee right? Kice living, but in prison?--Why in prison? Who told thee? Dost believe it? Art thou certain?
GANNAM	I heard say so no less a one than Kleib, Who bragged to-day about it in the street. For, hearing one lament the death of Kice, The Captain of the Guards, in churlish laughter, Gave out that Kice had been in prison since The war began; and none but he and Ahmed, Outside the prison, knew of it.
WAJDAH	Ahmed knew of it!?
GANNAM	Aye, Kleib had Ahmed's order in his hand, When he arrested Kice; and ever since He's held him prisoner in secrecy Imposed by Ahmed or Ali, or both. Now, I advise thee, Wajdah--O the hounds Are set--I saw them, heard them;--hie thee now To the Imam; appeal, implore, beseech. And if he hears thee not, I and a meager crew are at thy call. We'll buy with our own blood the life of Kice.

But now I must away. Seek thou Ali:
Seek him anon. And I shall come again
Before the day is done.

WAJDAH   Aye, come.

GANNAM   Farewell.

(Exit)

WAJDAH   Kice living, and in Koufah?--
In prison, and by Ahmed's order?--
And he comes here to plight his faith, his love?--
Holds Kice in prison, and conceals it from me?--
And lies to me?--Why?-- What is his design?--
O, can it be that he suspects--O Heaven!
Must I lose Kice again,
And having found him living?
Would he, who comes here wooing, reave me now
Of my son? Never, never! I have this.

(Feeling for her dagger)

But I must hasten to Ali.

(Goes towards door)

(Enter AHMED)

AHMED   Salaam, O Wajdah.

WAJDAH   (Recognizing his voice and turning abruptly) Ahmed here?
Ahmed in Wajdah's house?

AHMED   Didst thou not send for me?

WAJDAH   I did, I did.
But that was when thy name
Was still a balm to my heart
Was still a flower in my breast,
Was still a treacle on my tongue:

But now it tastes like colocynth,[1]
And I would none of it--I spit it out.
Thou void of manhood, faith and honor! Shame,
That on those lying lips a hair should grow.

AHMED   What means all this? why rate and chide me thus?

WAJDAH   Accursed! And dost thou still feign ignorance?
Dost come here still, and knowing that I know thee?
Go: from thy scurvy heart I turn my eyes--
I never knew that baseness had a heart
To make such feigns magnanimous of love.

AHMED   But hear me, Wajdah.

WAJDAH   No, I can not hear.--
Thy place--approach not further-answer me,
Where's Kice:

AHMED   Why calumniate me thus.

WAJDAH   Where's Kice?

AHMED   O Wajdah, calm thyself and hear, I pray.
O, deem me not so low; for if thou knew,
Thy life no longer being safe in Koufah,
I come to succor thee--

WAJDAH   Enough, enough!
I'd none of this. But tell me, where is Kice?
Canst thou not lie to me as is thy wont?
Art thou afraid of telling now the truth?

AHMED   Why should I lie, why should I be afraid?

WAJDAH   Then answer me, dost thou know aught of Kice?

---

1. A Mediterranean and African herbaceous vine.

AHMED	Kice is in prison.
WAJDAH	Eigh, in prison, he? And didst thou not know it, O my loving friend?
AHMED	O yes, I did.
WAJDAH	And oft as I inquired Of thee concerning him, thou, without shame Or hesitation, lied to me.
AHMED	But I Had orders to obey.
WAJDAH	Orders, thou sayst? Orders to come under my peaceful roof A traitor in the vernal guise of love? Orders to goal the fairest human flower And bring me with a tainted hand a branch Of falsehood's wilted myrtle in return? Orders to add such fuel to my woes, And witness all my anguish and my pain, Withholding all the while the anodyne, Which thou, if thou weret honest, shouldst have brought? A word had done it, churl,--a word which now Falls e'en reluctantly from thy foul lips. And yet, with brazen face and glozing tongue, Thou comest to exhibit here again Thy base and treacherous heart. Out on thee, churl!
AHMED	Art done? Wilt thou not hear me speak?
WAJDAH	No, not a word. Leave thou my house anon.
AHMED	O Wajdah, do not blindly thus misjudge me; Do not condemn before--
WAJDAH	Begone, I say.

AHMED	Let me explain--let me now tell the truth.
WAJDAH	Thou wilt compel me then to call my slaves.
	(As she moves toward the door, Ahmed stops her threateningly.)
AHMED	Thou wilt regret if in perversity--
	(Wajdah stands before him arms folded, and with a look of supreme contempt. He continues, changing his tone.)
	I beg of thee, O Wajdah, hear me.
	(She turns away from him, clapping her hands to her ears.)
WAJDAH	Speak.
AHMED	Must I recoil as from a viper now, Though, billah! I can crush thee. O, beware! I brooked enough. Thou hast in poisoned humor Chided and cursed and vilified a friend. Aye, spit on me, and turn me from they house. But if thou wert amenable to reason, If thou wert sane--a life were better saved.
	(Wajdah, claps for a servant.)
	No need to call thy slaves; I leave thee now. But know thou reprobate, thou wanton one That Kice will follow Mustafa, and soon.
	(Exit)
WAJDAH	And will he do it? Oh, I must be quick.
	(Re-enter SALWAH)
	If Gannam comes, let him await me here, Dost hear, O Salwah?-I shall soon return. I go to see my son, to save my son.
	(Exit)

CURTAIN

ACT IV

Scene I

A Hall in the House of the Khalif furnished with rugs and divans; armor hanging on the walls; brass lanterns hanging from the ceiling, which is of rafters; trophies, such as statues of horses and warriors made of gold, stand here and there. Doors double arched casement and double doors opening on a colonnaded corridor. Dim light. Towards evening.

AHMED   (Discovered) If thou but knew that I had come to save
       Thee and thy son!--But woe now to the twain.
       O cruel woman, I shall be avenged--
       But if I can persuade the Khalif--well--
       Then I can wash my hands--

       (Enter Ali with a number of turbaned Sheikhs)

ALI   (To Sheikhs) She must be out of Koufah by this time.

SHEIKHS   Allah be praised! And peace with thee, Imam.

       (Exeunt Sheikhs)

ALI   The peace of Allah--and his guidance too.
       (To Ahmed) Our order 's executed, is it not?

AHMED   May't please thee, I can say to this extent,
       That I have been to Wajdah's house myself
       To find out if thy message was received.

ALI   And was it not?

AHMED   It was.

ALI   And is she now
       Departed?

AHMED   She is not.

ALI	But why?
AHMED	Her son--
ALI	(Impatiently) And what about her son?
AHMED	It's for his sake That she remains.
ALI	(Angrily) Eigh! what! Is he again--
AHMED	(Suavely) May't please thee--
ALI	Stop: has not our order then Been executed?
AHMED	No.
ALI	(Perturbed) Why not, why not?
AHMED	Because the rancor of the people 's reached The gaols, and even the guards and gaolers now Are clamoring for Kice's life and Wajdah's.
ALI	And the Khalif's, too, the Khalif's life, why not?-- The voice of hell is in the people's voice, When with inhuman leathern throat it howls Against a life which only one can judge. The brain-sick people! think they in this garb Allah hath placed a shadow of a Khalif!
AHMED	Their disaffection thou wilt not invite.
ALI	Must I their fiendish rancor humor now? Can I not ever further a just cause Without displeasing the beloved people? The faithless, blind, perverse and fickle people, Must I before them mumble, smirk and beg? What is their disaffection in the scale

Which justice balances and mercy holds?
God of the Ḳaaba! the sandal which I clout
With my own hand, is of more worth to me,
Yea, than this Khalifate, if I can not
Even with a word crush down an evil thing
And uphold Allah's justice, Allah's truth.

AHMED   And might there not be justice in their cause?
          Was not Mustafa executed for
          The very crime that hangs round Kice's neck?

ALI   Even so, but the war is over now.
          And in the fair security of peace
          It right becomes the Prophet's followers
          To be forgiving. Go thyself, therefore,
          And execute my order--go at once:
          Let Kice and Wajdah now depart in peace.

AHMED   May't please thee, Imam, but she might be now
          In the hands of the enraged multitudes;
          And such attempts as I might make to save
          Her, even with a body of the guards--

ALI   Fellow, thou speakest like a zealot now.

AHMED   I speak the truth.

ALI   The truth, my foolish boy?
          The truth can never live in venomed hearts,
          The truth has never come from poisoned lips.--
          Go, do my bidding, and no more of this.

AHMED   I go to do my best.

          (Exit)

ALI   The multitudes,
          I must now bow before the multitudes,
          And kiss their hands, and hearken to their will.

Bah! A fury fanned by the fanatic sheikhs,
Who lie, and cry "apostate", and abet
The sheep to join in the howling with the wolves.

(Enter ABBAS, ABU-MOUSA and others)

What news, Abbas?

ABBAS   She's by the crowd pursued.

ALI   By Allah and the Prophet! I myself

Will rescue her.

(Going)

ABBAS   Beware, Ali!
Thy life 's in danger too.

ABU-MOUSA In truth, Imam,
Koufah 's against us now.

ALI   And I'm against
Koufah. Mouse-minded menials, I alone--

ABBAS   But all the soldiery, in truth--

ALI   Enough!
Hear me, hear Ali, if you'd know the truth.
She whom now Koufah persecutes has done
More good to Koufah than the best of men;
She whom the Moslem people would cut off,
Has given a whole kingdom to Islam;
She whom our sheikhs and zealots call apostate,
Has done heroic deeds in Allah's name.
And this--(Striking his left arm with his hand)
If you but knew it, O, ye Arabs,
Who hold the sacrament of brotherhood
Dearer than human life, if you but knew!--(Bearing his arm.)
Now, would you have me execute a friend,

One who once sucked a snake-bite on this arm?
She who has saved my life, would I take hers?
By Allah and the Prophet, never, never!
And if Mohammed is the thunderbolt (Tumult within.)
Of Allah's wrath, remember he is, too,
The rainbow of his clemency and love.

(Enter WAJDAH, pursued by the multitudes)

WAJDAH   (Appealing to ALI.) O, let them wait until I see my son.

ALI   Vale your weapons! Shame on you--stand back!

CITIZEN   The Prophet says, A sword on the apostate.

              (The same repeated by the crowd.)

ALI   (With calm persuasion) But Allah says, Be merciful.

              (A commotion among the crowd. Some are heard asking,
              "Is't so, is't so?", while others nod and make gestures of
              approval. They sheathe, therefore, their swords and recede.
              Wajdah is standing near Ali; Abu-Mousa and Abbas showing
              amazement.)

                              Tableau

              And this intrusion on the privacy
              Of the Khalif is forgiven. Nay, speak not.
              I hear no grievances within my house;
              Await me in the court below--I come.
              Go with them Abu-Mousa and Abbas.

              (Exeunt Abbas, Abu-Mousa and Crowd)

              (Ali opens door and conducts Wajdah to it.)

              Await me here; soon thou shalt see thy son.

              (Exit Wajdah)

              (Just then Ahmed is seen and withdraws until Ali goes out.)

              By Allah, they can have the Khalifate
              And every drop that runs within these veins,
              (Clapping his hand to his neck)
              But not a drop of hers, no, never, never!

(Exit)

(Enter Ahmed)

AHMED   I'll give thee one more chance. (Goes to door)
For thine own sake,
O Wajdah, one more chance. Yea, I hold out
A friendly hand--I open to thee again
The door of life, of freedom, and of love
(He opens the door.)
O Wajdah, come; make haste now; come, make haste.

(Enter WAJDAH, who is startled at seeing AHMED)

WAJDAH   Thou?

AHMED   But not of the multitude am I.

WAJDAH   And what wouldst thou? Why still pursuest me?

AHMED   I come again to save thee.

WAJDAH   I thank thee.
Who hath the master's sword needs not the slave's.

AHMED   But art thou certain that thy master's sword
Can serve thy freedom now? Hear that. Come, see.
He can not even calm the multitudes,
My master and thy savior.--Hear me, Wajdah:
I beg thee, I entreat thee, come with me;
For by and Arab's troth, I come to save thee.

WAJDAH   And by my god, thou art presumptuous too;
For how canst thou, if the Imam can not.

AHMED   I have devised some means. O, trust in me:--
O, haste thee now, for in a trice the crowd
Will be within the house,--and all is lost!

WAJDAH   No, no; I had as lief a martyr die.

94

AHMED	And wouldst thou also sacrifice thy son? Wouldst thou not see him?
WAJDAH	I would have thee know That in this house I've no disquietude. I seek not nor thy counsel nor thine aid. Begone, I've done with thee.
AHMED	(Earnestly) For thy son's sake Be not so blindly, fatally perverse; Once more I offer thee a friendly hand, The hand of faithfulness, devotion, love!
WAJDAH	A guilty hand! Life were a curse from such.
AHMED	(Drawing his sword in a flash of temper) And this.
WAJDAH	And dost thou dare!
AHMED	If from this hand Life be a curse, then death is a blessing. Exit in haste.
WAJDAH	(About to call him back, but changes her mind.) What do I want with him? The Khalif said I soon shall see my son. The Khalif's word Is law.--But where is Ahmed gone!--His threat Is not to kill himself, I hope.--But whom (With sudden realization) My god, my god! (Runs to the door) He's gone.--(Pauses confused) A foolish thought. But when he drew his sword I read in his eyes A treacherous, a murderous intent. Ahmed, Ahmed! (Claps one hand upon the other in despair) He's gone -- he's gone to--bah! (Makes a gesture as if chasing from before her eyes the specter of evil thought; and then, with calm assurance)

I'm in the house of Imam Ali now:
No harm can come to those whom he protects.

(Enter ALI, followed by KLEIB and GUARDS)

ALI   (Looking out of casement)
The storm is now subsided; all is well.
(Coming down stage)
Make haste, O Wajdah, go now with the guards,
Who will conduct thee to the prison, where
Thou'lt see thy son, and then,--trust thee in Kleib.
He has my orders. (To Kleib) understand me well,
She is thy prisoner, but ere the sun
Pours to this wanten, undeserving city
Another cup of light, both she and Kice,
Under your own protection, should be sped
Away from Koufah,

KLEIB   To hear is to obey.

ALI   Farewell O Wajdah!
I hope that thou wilt soon be breathing again
The air of fair security and peace.

WAJDAH   I kiss thy hand in honest thankfulness,
(She kisses his hand, and he bends his head over her shoulder
and kisses it.)
And in the wilderness of my dark lot,
The flower of gratitude shall ever blow
To whisper Ali's name. Farewell.

ALI   (Pointing to heaven) Be thankful unto him,
In whose assurance thou art sped. Farewell.

(Exit WAJDAH, guarded and followed by KLEIB)

Drop.

Scene II

The Prison. Drop with three or four doors, one of which is practicable.

(Knocking at door)

Enter OBEID

OBEID	And who be this?
KLEIB	(Outside) Unbolt, Obeid, unbolt.
OBEID	(Unbolting door) What can the purpose of HIS visit be? (Enter GUARDS with flaming palm branches, WAJDAH among them, followed by KLEIB.) OBEID, as he sees them, recedes in amazement.
KLEIB	(To Guards) Guard ye the door outside. (To Obeid) The Khalif's order.
OBEID	More of the Khalif's orders, Allah 's great. (Reading) Life of the Prophet! this is very strange. (Pointing to Wajdah) And who 's the woman?
KLEIB	Mother of the prisoner.
OBEID	(Aside) I'm sorry for her sake.--I can not, Kleib, Obey this order of the Khalif.
KLEIB	Why?
OBEID	Having obeyed the previous one.
KLEIB	Which one?
OBEID	The one that Ahmed brought a while ago.
WAJDAH	(Perturbed) As I suspected.

KLEIB	(Concerned) And is he still here?
OBEID	He must be here somewhere
WAJDAH	(Impatiently) And where is Kice?
OBEID	What wouldst thou with him more?
WAJDAH	What dost thou mean?
OBEID	(With cynical indifference) I mean that --gug, gug, gug-- (Passing his hand across his throat) (KLEIB shakes his head mournfully.) Thus flowed his blood.
WAJDAH	(Beating her cheeks) O cruel, cruel heaven! Who ordered it--who ordered Kice's death?
OBEID	Didst thou not hear me say? The Khalif did. His order was brought by Ahmed himself.
WAJDAH	The treacherous one, the cursed lying one! The Khalif's order, he has even forged. O villain face, if I but see thee more!-- That is what I suspected--lack-a-day! They slew thee ere I knew thee...lack-a-day! Oh, let me see him, gaoler, let me see him.
OBEID	What wouldst thou see in a blood-dripping corpse?
WAJDAH	Oh, let me see him.
KLEIB	(To Obeid) Let her see her son.
OBEID	Come hither; (Goes to door and opens it) there's thy son. Nay, go not in.
WAJDAH	But I must see him.
KLEIB	Bring him out, Obeid.

OBEID	Come, then, thy hand. (They go in and bring out the body on a stretcher made of boards. It is covered with a tunic.)
VOICE	(Within) Obeid, Obeid.
OBEID	Hear that. As if Obeid were made of wood or stone! These sons of mischief will not let him rest. Exit
WAJDAH	(Falling near the body, uncovers the face.) O cloven, blossom-laden branch of youth, O well-beloved, thou art comely still. Thy smile, despite this hideous savage gash, Is living yet upon thy ruby lips;-- They are yet red as pomegranate flowers. (She covers his face with kisses, sobbing convulsively. Kleib turns his head sadly and goes out) Oh, spirit of my anguish, who be thou? (Takes up his right arm) The sign, the sign--is there a sign--not here-- (Takes up the other) And here--art thou the son of Wajdah? (Lifts her head and hands up to heaven, and in an expression of mingled joy and grief) No! O my beloved stranger, O slain love! In life, my soul has trembled round thy heart; In death, my heart weeps blood around thy soul. Oh, let me here (kissing him in the neck) now purify these lips; For once I thought I knew thee, and would not Know that I knew thee; --I would not repent. O, love born of the distant depths of light! O giver of the light that calms and guides!

Wouldst thou the earthen lamp that Wajdah brings
Fill now with blood instead of oil? O love,
Thy smile illuminates the world! O love,
Thy word the sun and moon obey! O love,
Thy silence flowers upon the path of men.
But wouldst thou turn they face forever now
From Wajdah's cracking heart,
From Wajdah's tear-drowned eyes?
And what is Wajdah but a speck of dust
Upon the highway of the gods? And yet,
A speck of dust that knows
That night is not the end--
Silence not the end:
The silence and the darkness are beginnings!--
Yes, yes, I know the meaning in thine eyes:
Look not beseeching, thou shalt be avenged.
See this. (Taking out her dagger) and passing it over his lips.)
O kiss it, kiss it, Kice. I shall
Not leave this city till I find him, yea,
And give thee satisfaction.

(Enter AHMED and is startled at seeing WAJDAH)

What! so soon?
The gods have never been so kind to me.

(Rushes at Ahmed and stabs him.)

AHMED   Akhs! Cruel to the last!
           (Staggers and falls.)

WAJDAH   'T is done, 't is done.
           O Kice, look at me now:

           (Kneels over the body)
           art thou content?
           Give me, therefore, to help me to endure,
           A token of this holy calm of death
           Enthroned upon thy brow; another from
           The living flowers of love upon thy lips;
           And still another from the soul of pain
           That lingers in this gash upon thy neck.

Oh, with these treasures I shall seek a place
Of solitude remote, where none can hear,
When every evening till the end of my days,
I sing my dirges to the night and stars.

(She hears the groans of Ahmed and turns of a sudden.)

AHMED   Oh, help me.

WAJDAH   Felon, were I cruel, I
            Would leave thee to the torments of slow death.

            (Rises with dagger in hand.)

AHMED   Oh, pity, pity, Wajdah.

            (She is about to strike him again, but withholds as she
            perceives the tattoo marks on his arm raised toward her in
            supplication.)

WAJDAH   What is this?

            (Throws down the dagger, and, taking up his arm, gazes at the
            sign.)

AHMED   Oh, Wajdah, --I am dying--but not--my love--

WAJDAH   But tell me of this mark, I beg thee, speak.

AHMED   My slayer begs?

WAJDAH   I beg, beseech thee, speak.

AHMED   It is a charm--a picture--of the charm--
            My mother--hung--around my neck--when a child--
            My servant Gannam--used to say--

            (Wajdah dumbstricken digs her hands into her hair and claps
            her face on the ground as if burying her head in the dust. For a
            moment she is impassive, still as a stone, and then she bursts
            out in convulsive weeping).

AHMED   Oh, Oh,--I'm dying.

             (She takes up his head and kisses him on the brow. He falls
             dead in her arms. She kisses him again and again; and then,
             kneeling as she is between the two bodies, turns from one to
             the other and falls again into a sort of stupor, burying her head
             in the dust. A moment, and she swings around, searching for
             the dagger. She finds it and is about to strike herself when she
             hears the voice of the Muazzen in the distance.)

MUAZZEN   (Calling the Faithful to the evening prayer.)
             Allahu akbar!

WAJDAH   (Turning her face towards the voice)
             Call thou the multitude--let them behold
             My son's blood, and my love's blood, and my own--

MUAZZEN   **Allahu akbar!**

WAJDAH   (Throwing away the dagger) No; I must not die--
             I'm not deserving of thy bounty, death.
             For Kice's sake and Ahmed's I must live;
             But where away, alas, where shall I go?

MUAZZEN   **La ilaha illallah, la ilaha illallah!**

             (Wajdah, her face still turned in the direction of the
             Muazzen's voice, uplifts her hands and bows three times,
             repeating the words,
             GOD IS ALMIGHTY, GOD IS ALL!)

             CURTAIN

The English Works of Ameen F. Rihani

Essays

1. THE WHITE WAY AND THE DESERT, Ms.[1], 1898-1939, ARMA[2] and LOC[3].

2. LETTERS TO UNCLE SAM, Ms., 1917-1919, ARMA and LOC.

3. THE PATH OF VISION, 1921; James T. White Co., New York. Reprinted 1970, Beirut, Lebanon. Refer to ARTW[4].

4. THE PAN ARAB MOVEMENT, Ms., 1930, ARMA and LOC.

5. THE FATE OF PALESTINE, 1967 [posth.], The Rihani Printing and Publishing House, Beirut, Lebanon. Refer to ARTW.

Historical and Political Analysis

6. TURKEY AND ISLAM IN THE WAR, Ms., 1915-1917, ARMA and LOC.

7. THE DESCENT OF BOLCHEVISM, 1920, The Stratford Co., Boston, USA. Refer to ARTW.

8. MAKER OF MODERN ARABIA or IBN SAOUD OF ARABIA, HIS PEOPLE AND HIS LAND, 1928, Constable and Co., Ltd., London, England; Houghton Mifflin Co., Boston, USA; Macmillan Co., Toronto, Canada; and Oxford University Press, Bombay, Calcutta and Madras, India, Reprinted 1933, London, Boston, Toronto, Bombay, Calcutta and Madras; 1983, New York.

9. IRAQ DURING THE DAYS OF KING FAISAL THE FIRST, Ms., 1932, ARMA and LOC.

---

1. Ms. = Manuscript.
2. ARMA = Ameen Rihani Museum Archives (Freike, Lebanon).
3. LOC = Library of Congress (Washington, DC, U.S.A.).
4. ARTW = Ameen Rihani's Translated Works.

Literary Criticism

10. CRITIQUES IN ART, 1999, [posth.], Librairie Du Liban Publishers, Beirut, Lebanon.

11. THE LORE OF THE ARABIAN NIGHTS, Ms., 1929, ARMA and LOC.

12. ARABIAN CONTRIBUTION TO CIVILIZATION, Ms., 1930, ARMA and LOC.

13. THE POETRY OF ARABIA, Ms., 1930, ARMA and LOC.

Novels, Short Stories and Plays

14. WAJDAH, 2001, [posth.], Platform International, Washington, DC, USA.

15. THE BOOK OF KHALID, 1911, Dodd Mead and Co., New York, USA. Reprinted 1973 and 2000, Beirut, Lebanon. Refer to ARTW.

16. THE GREEN FLAG, Ms., 1911-1921, ARMA and LOC.

17. THE LILY OF AL-GHORE, Ms., 1914, ARMA and LOC. Refer to ARTW.

18. JAHAN, Ms., 1917, ARMA and LOC. Refer to ARTW.

19. DOCTOR DELLA VALLE, Ms., 1918, ARMA and LOC.

Poetry

20. THE QUATRAINS OF ABUL-'ALA', 1903, Doubleday Page and Co., New York, USA.

21. MYRTLE AND MYRRH, 1905, Gorham Press, Boston, USA.

22. THE LUZUMIYAT OF ABUL-'ALA', 1918, James T. White and Co., New York, USA. Reprinted 1920, New York; 1944 and 1978, Beirut, Lebanon.

23. A CHANT OF MYSTICS AND OTHER POEMS, 1921, James T. White and Co., New York, USA. Reprinted 1970, Beirut, Lebanon.

24. THE THIRD POETRY COLLECTION, Ms., 1897-1937, ARMA and LOC.

Travel

25. IN THE LAND OF THE MAYAS, Ms., 1918-1919, ARMA and LOC.

26. ARABIAN PEAK AND DESERT, 1931, Constable and Co., London, England; Macmillan Co., Toronto, Canada; The Oxford University Press, Bombay, Calcutta and Madras, India. Reprinted 1931, Houghton Mifflin Co., Boston; 1933, London, Toronto, Boston, Bombay, Calcutta and Madras; 1983, New York.

27. AROUND THE COASTS OF ARABIA, 1930, Consdtable and Co., London, England; Macmillan Co., Toronto, Canada; The Oxford University Press, Bombay, Calcutta and Madras, India. Reprinted 1931, Houghton Mifflin Co., Boston; 1933, London, Toronto, Boston, Bombay, Calcutta and Madras; 1983, New York.

28. KURDISTAN, Ms., 1932, ARMA and LOC.

Letters

29. THE ENGLISH LETTERS OF AMEEN RIHANI, Ms. 1897-1940, ARMA and LOC.